# THE COSTUME BOOK FOR PARTIES

## AND PLAYS

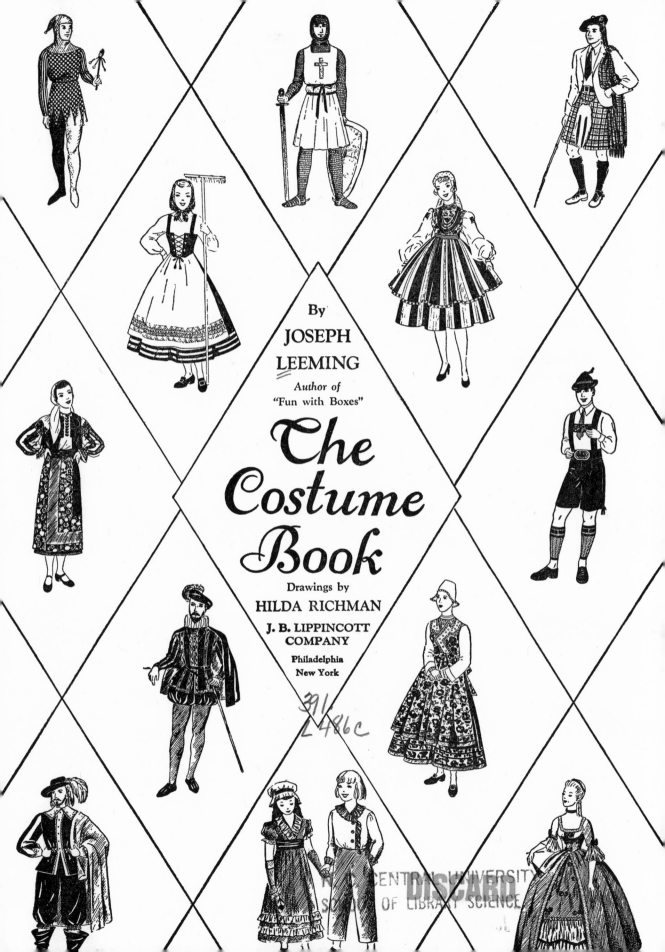

By
JOSEPH
LEEMING

Author of
"Fun with Boxes"

# The Costume Book

Drawings by
HILDA RICHMAN

J. B. LIPPINCOTT
COMPANY

Philadelphia
New York

ISBN-0-397-30043-3

Library of Congress catalog card number 38-27654

*Printed in the United States of America*

FOR
AVERY

# CONTENTS

## PART I
## NATIONAL FOLK COSTUMES

## PART II
## HISTORIC COSTUMES

## PART III
## SPECIAL COSTUMES

# INDEX

Use this list as suggestions for party costumes, as well as for
finding costume descriptions

· xiv ·

# FOREWORD

THE folk-costumes of the Old World countries are infinitely varied. In many of the countries, each district or province has it distinctive dress, and in some countries even the villages have costumes that possess some special, zealously retained characteristics. In addition to these factors, the individual taste of the wearer brings about many variations in material, color, and design, and in many countries, there are special costumes for different occasions and classes, for weddings, for mourning, for single and married women, and so on.

For this reason, it is difficult to pick out the one costume that typifies the national dress of each country. In most instances, however, the general folk dress of each country is marked by certain well-defined characteristics. No one, for example, would ever confuse the dress of the Dutch Volendammer, with its baggy trousers, with the neat short-trousered costume worn by the men of the Austrian Tyrol. Few of the European folk costumes are as exaggeratedly different as these two. The differences are considerably less noticeable, but they exist nevertheless.

Folk costumes in all countries are nearly always the same for the children as for the adults and the costumes illustrated are those worn by children as well as adults.

In addition to the folk costumes, every effort has been made to include the principal costumes, historical and fanciful, that are needed in plays frequently given by amateurs, as well as for parties and pageants. As this outline of costumes is necessarily brief and covers only the most outstanding types of garments, for further details concerning the dress of the different periods, a valuable reference work is recommended: "Historic Costume," by Katherine M. Lester.

Well-known book-character costumes—such as those of Alice in Wonderland, the Duchess, the Queen of Hearts, Little Lord Fauntleroy, Rip Van Winkle, Tom Sawyer and Little Black Sambo—have not been described in the text since they are easily reproduced by following the illustrations in these familiar books, with the help of the principles of the art of "make-it-yourself" costuming, explained in this volume.

# THE COSTUME BOOK FOR PARTIES

## AND PLAYS

# HOW TO MAKE COSTUMES AT HOME

PRACTICALLY all of the costumes described in the following pages can be made at home very easily. Even those that look most "foreign" or elaborate can be reproduced, wholly or in part, by making minor alterations in common American garments that are already in one's possession. Pyjamas, in their original form or slightly altered, to cite only one example, are suitable for literally dozens of peasant and historical garments.

While the total effect of a costume may be bewilderingly exotic, it should be remembered that it is simply a combination of fundamental garments. For men, these are, of course, trousers, shirts, vests, and jackets or coats; while for women, they are chiefly skirts, blouses, and bodices or corselets. Let us consider these various garments.

In the men's or boys' costumes, most of the long trousers illustrated can be made from cheap cotton or khaki trousers, or pyjama trousers, either cotton or flannel. If the trousers are fairly close-fitting, as in the Mexican or Indian costume, it will be necessary to take out some of the material, a relatively simple operation. Tights, or hose, such as those worn by the men of the Elizabethan period, can be made from women's long stockings, from long winter underwear, or by using a union suit. If the latter is used, but is to be dyed, it is wise to have it a little larger than necessary, as it may shrink during the dyeing.

Knee-breeches, particularly of the close-fitting type required for the Spanish, Norwegian and American Colonial costumes, can also be made from flannel pyjama trousers, cut off to the proper length and dyed the desired color. The fuller knee-breeches, such as those worn by the men of Italy and Sweden, can be reproduced with golf knickerbockers that are not too baggy, or with boys' knickerbockers. For the very full knee-breeches worn by the Hollanders of Marken and the men of Brittany, girls' gymnasium bloomers are admirably suitable.

The men's vests are chiefly of two types, those cut exactly or nearly like the ordinary man's vest, and those that button close round the neck. The former can be reproduced by covering an ordinary vest with material of the required color, which in most cases is red, blue or green. In a few of the costumes, the vest of this type buttons quite close to the neck. This effect can be obtained by adding an extra button above the regular buttons. The high, round-necked type of vest can be reproduced by remodeling a pyjama top. Cut the sleeves off and remove enough material from the back of the garment to make it fit snugly around the body. Then dye the cloth or cover it with material of the desired color and add the two or more rows of buttons that are called for in the costume.

The short jackets, either with or without sleeves, that are needed for some of the costumes, can in many cases be made from men's vests as just described. If sleeves are required they will, of course, have to be added to the vest. Bolero jackets with rounded corners can be modeled from the indispensable pyjama top if one does not wish to make them.

Only a few of the men's costumes, such as those of the Irishman and the Colonial American, call for long tail-coats. When such a garment is needed, the best plan is to get one of the patterns that are sold in any pattern department. Ask for the pattern for a Colonial costume.

At first glance, the women's skirts called for by many costumes seem to vary considerably, and some of them, especially the very voluminous ones, may appear difficult to reproduce. The very large skirts, such as those of the Volendam and Czechoslovakian women, are really several skirts worn over each other. A simple way to achieve their effect, is to make the underskirts from crepe paper. The other skirts should present no difficulty to anyone who is in the least familiar with simple dressmaking.

The tight-laced bodices that are so picturesque a part of many of the women's costumes can be easily made from a single piece of material. Dyed muslin, flannelette, or black cambric (dull side out) are suitable. The bodice is cut to fit around the waist of the wearer and button holes are made in it to accommodate the lacing ribbons. The bodices can be strengthened considerably by lining them with buckram.

## Patterns

Simple patterns for a number of the most commonly used garments mentioned in the text are shown on the opposite page.

With these as guides, cut full-sized patterns from newspaper,

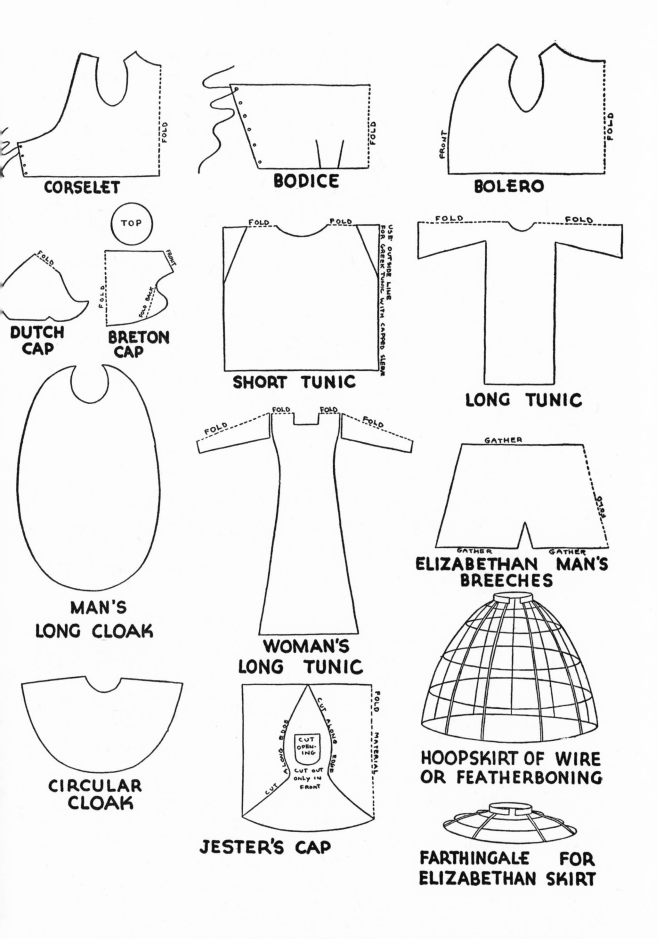

**CORSELET**

**BODICE**

**BOLERO**

FRONT
FOLD

**DUTCH CAP**

FOLD

TOP

**BRETON CAP**

FOLD
FOLD
FRONT
FOLD BACK

**SHORT TUNIC**

FOLD
FOLD
USE OUTSIDE LINE FOR GREEK TUNIC WITH CAPPED SLEEVE

**LONG TUNIC**

FOLD
FOLD

**MAN'S LONG CLOAK**

**WOMAN'S LONG TUNIC**

FOLD
FOLD
FOLD
FOLD

**ELIZABETHAN MAN'S BREECHES**

GATHER
FOLD
GATHER
GATHER

**CIRCULAR CLOAK**

**JESTER'S CAP**

CUT ALONG EDGE
CUT ALONG EDGE
CUT OPENING
CUT OUT ONLY IN FRONT
CUT ALONG EDGE
FOLD MATERIAL

**HOOPSKIRT OF WIRE OR FEATHERBONING**

**FARTHINGALE FOR ELIZABETHAN SKIRT**

starting with waist or head measurement, as the case may be, and following the general proportions shown in the guide. Lay the pattern on the person to wear it, and cut till it fits.

The basic patterns will require certain slight modifications to adapt them to the particular costume. For instance, when making the short Greek tunic, the shoulder seam should be left partly open in order to make the capped sleeve, while for the medieval peasant's tunic which has long sleeves, it is better to use the pattern for the long tunic, shortening it as desired.

When making home-made costumes, the aim should be to produce strong but not necessarily permanent garments. In other words, do not spend too much time making fine stitches that in all probability will never be seen or appreciated. Most costumes are designed to be worn only a few times and there is no need to toil over them as though they were Sunday gowns. They are fun to make, if they are not taken too seriously.

### *Materials*

A number of inexpensive materials are available, that imitate the fabrics used in the original costumes.

Silks and satins can be imitated by using glazed cambric, silkoline or rayon. Deep-colored canton flannel makes an excellent substitute for velvet. Where brocades are called for, use heavy cretonne or cotton tapestry. Brocades and embroidery can also be imitated by pasting crepe paper designs on cloth or on crepe paper if the costume is made of that material.

Linen can be represented by muslin, and woolen garments can be reproduced with woolen batiste, canton flannel, flannelette, heavy muslin, or even cambric, with the dull side out. Other materials that will be found useful for many of the costumes are calico, percale, cheese-cloth and sateen. Cheese-cloth is the material to use for Grecian tunics and for fairy garments.

Many of the costumes described can be made either in whole or in part from crepe paper. This material has the advantage of being inexpensive and it is surprisingly durable. It can be handled just as one would handle a fabric, and can be either sewed or pasted together. The one all-important rule to remember when using crepe paper is that to hang correctly it must be used *with the grain going up and down.*

# Part I
# NATIONAL FOLK COSTUMES

# ARABIA

THE picturesque costumes of the Arabs are designed to provide protection against the intense heat of the deserts and at the same time keep out the wind-blown sand. There is a good deal of variety in Arab dress, but the fundamental garments composing the costume are nearly always the same. The costume is the one to use for a Sheik of Araby, either for a play or a party.

The man wears loose, wide trousers, but these cannot be seen, as they are covered by the *kamis,* a long cotton robe that reaches from the neck to the ankles and is girdled at the waist with a broad sash. This garment is fastened by a row of buttons that extends from the waist to the round, close-fitting collar. Frequently, the *kamis* is white, but it may also be of striped or figured material. One way to reproduce it is to use an old-fashioned night shirt.

Over the *kamis* is worn a long, flowing coat-like garment that reaches to the ground. This is the *kaftan.* Formerly it was made of rich brocades and satins; nowadays it may be of wool or cotton. Generally, it is black or dark brown in color, though sometimes it is red or blue or of striped material. It can be reproduced, for costume purposes, by using a bath gown or dressing gown.

The Arabs' footgear consists of yellow or red leather slippers or thick-soled sandals. The headdress, called the *kufiyah,* is distinctive, and consists of a large kerchief bound to the head by one or two *agals,* circles of wool wound with gold or silver threads. These can be made by sewing gold or silver cloth around a strip of twisted cloth shaped to form a circle.

For characters in Arabian Nights plays, such as Ali Baba or Sinbad, the usual costume consists of long white or colored trousers or bloomers, a white or colored shirt with a round neck and very full sleeves, a broad sash and a short bolero jacket or a long flowing cloak or *kaftan.* A turban is worn instead of the desert headdress.

The Arab woman wears full, ankle-length trousers that are generally made of richly-colored brocade, satin, or velvet. Full pyjama trousers are just the thing to use for a costume. These are almost entirely hidden by the *gondura,* a loose muslin or calico robe that reaches to the ankles. This may be white, solid-colored, or of gayly striped material, and can be best reproduced by using a dressing gown.

ARABIA

Over the *gondura* is thrown a loose wrap, the *shale*. This is frequently of black silk embroidered around the edges with gold or silver threads.

The head is covered by the *haik,* a loose white veil that is almost invariably embroidered with metallic threads. Red or yellow slippers with pointed toes are worn.

For further details of the more elaborate Arabian and Oriental costumes suitable for Arabian Nights plays and Oriental pageants, the following books will be found helpful:

*Oriental Costumes,* Max Tilke; *The Arabian Nights,* Edited by Kate Douglas Wiggin and Nora A. Smith, illustrated by Maxfield Parrish; *The Arabian Nights,* Olcott; *Omar Khayyam,* illustrated by Elihu Vedder. *See also the section in this book on Turkey.*

## AUSTRIA

THERE is no other place in western Europe where the wearing of the native costumes has continued so persistently as in the Austrian Tyrol. Even today, the traditional costumes are worn every day in many sections, including those that are seldom visited by tourists. The Tyrolean costumes that have been selected for description are among the most picturesque in all of Europe. It should be noted that the clothes worn by the men are practically identical with those worn by the Swiss. For either a party, or a play such as "Heidi," the men's costume described may be considered as authentic for both Austria and Switzerland.

In the original costume, the trousers are made of chamois skin which is either black or dark blue in color. Two kinds of trousers are worn, close-fitting shorts that leave the knees bare, and breeches that button around and below the knee. Flannel pyjama trousers are suggested for reproducing both kinds. The trousers are held up by broad blue, black, or green suspenders. These cross in the back and the two straps in the front are joined by a cross piece, that is frequently embroidered. A broad black leather belt of the type shown in the drawing is also used.

Heavy white or gray woolen stockings are commonly worn, but many of the Tyroleans use footless stockings that reach from the knee to just above the ankle.

A soft white shirt is worn with a narrow red or black tie. Over

TYROLEAN

# AUSTRIA

this is a high-necked red waistcoat. This can be made from a flannel pyjama top by cutting off the collar and sleeves. A short, collarless blue jacket completes the costume. This is most easily reproduced by covering a man's vest with dark blue material. Silver buttons should be sewed to each side in the front and on the cuffs of the sleeves. If you have no Alpine hat, you can fake one by folding the crown of a girl's felt hat into a peak and adding a feather.

The Tyrolean girl's or woman's dress is very simple to make. The short skirt, which comes to just below the knees, is bright red in color. Over it is a white apron of almost the same length. Two or three bands of blue or green material are typical and may be sewed to the apron near its bottom edge. The stockings are white.

The blouse is of white cotton and has short rather full sleeves. The Tyrolean women wear blouses with several different types of sleeves, and there is no single pattern that is definitely predominant. The sleeves are both short and long, and may be either plain or puffed. Almost invariably they are finished with one or more frills at the elbow or wrist.

Outside the blouse there is a tight-fitting corselet made of red material edged with blue. (For pattern, see page 5.) Beneath the lacing there is a slip of gayly-colored pleated or gathered silk. Kerchiefs and richly embroidered shawls are very frequently worn by the women of the Tyrol and may be appropriately used in connection with the costume described.

## CHINA

THE most gorgeous costumes of China were the richly embroidered robes of the mandarins and their wives. These were done away with when the republic was established in 1912, and the Chinese officials now wear European dress.

Drawings of a Chinese mandarin and his wife in their official robes are provided as a guide for those who wish to reproduce these costumes. The mandarin's underskirt is embroidered with characteristic Chinese designs. The wide-sleeved covering robe is dark colored, blue, gray or black, and has a large piece of embroidery, almost a foot square, on the front and back. This showed, by its design, to which branch of the government service the wearer belonged. A wild animal indicated the army or navy, while a bird showed that the wearer was in the civil service. The hat can be

MANDARIN
AND
WIFE

CITIZEN
AND
WIFE

# CHINA

reproduced by sewing cloth over a cardboard or buckram foundation. The upturned brim should be brown to imitate fur, and the crown is pink. On the very top there is a round button. It is black or blue, with a gold edging, and has a peacock feather attached to it which hangs down over the back of the neck. The shoes are the distinctive Chinese slippers which can be purchased nowadays in many American stores.

The costume of the mandarin's wife is very similar to that of her husband. One or two embroidered underskirts are worn and are covered by a robe cut as shown in the drawing.

The daily costume of the ordinary Chinaman is much the same as that worn at the time of the empire. The trousers are long and very full, and may be blue, black, or white. The stockings are white and are worn with Chinese slippers.

The upper part of the body is covered by a short, dark blue jacket. It has a standing collar and full sleeves and is fastened across the front of the chest with buttons and loops. It can be reproduced from an ordinary pyjama top.

It is not generally known that the Chinaman's queue, or pig-tail, was worn by order of his Manchu conquerors as a sign of submission. It has not been generally worn since the passing of the Manchu empire in 1912, but can be used, of course, for costume purposes. The most commonly used hat is the round black skull cap shown in the drawing. It can be reproduced by sewing black cloth over a circular cardboard or buckram foundation.

Chinese women wear the hair with bangs in front, drawn straight back and fastened in a knot at the nape of the neck.

The Chinese women wear trousers, like the men, but they are not so full. Pyjama trousers will serve admirably. The favorite color for all parts of the women's costume is blue, but black and gray, as well as lighter colors such as green and pink, are also widely used. White stockings and Chinese slippers peep out from beneath the woman's trousers. In North China the trousers are tied at the ankles, but in South China they are left unconfined.

Over the upper part of her body, the woman wears a knee length or shorter coat, called the *ma-coual*. It has wide sleeves and a narrow standing collar and is buttoned up the right side. Its color is sometimes the same as that of the trousers, and sometimes a contrasting shade.

Out-of-doors the Chinese woman wears a long, wide-sleeved robe, or *haol,* of the type shown in the drawing. Generally it is of dark blue or black silk. If included in the costume, the robe will probably have to be made in its entirety, as it does not resemble any commonly worn Western garment.


## CZECHOSLOVAKIA

MANY varied costumes are found in Czechoslovakia, which includes within its borders the old provinces of Bohemia, Moravia, Silesia, and Slovakia. The general characteristics of the costumes worn in the different sections of the country are roughly similar. The men wear either tight-fitting long trousers or knee-breeches tucked into high soft leather boots, white shirts and bolero type jackets. The women's costumes are characterized by voluminous medium-length skirts worn over a number of petticoats or underskirts, and blouses with very distinctive puffed sleeves. The costumes of both sexes are noteworthy for their brilliant coloring and extraordinarily rich embroidery.

The man's costume illustrated is the one worn in Moravia. It is the most picturesque of the native Czechoslovakian costumes. The breeches are of dark blue material and are decorated with embroidery from the waist a short distance down each leg. They can be made by dyeing an old pair of linen golf trousers, or even a pair of pyjama trousers, blue and sewing on strips of figured crepe for the embroidery. If high black boots such as those shown in the drawing are not available, the trousers may be made to reach to the ankle. In this case, they should be made quite tight-fitting and each leg should be narrower at the ankle than at the knee. With this kind of trousers, black shoes are worn.

The white linen shirt is noteworthy because of its very full puffed sleeves. There is a band of embroidery in front where the shirt buttons and the collar is also embroidered. Crepe paper can be used to reproduce this effect.

The bolero, or sleeveless jacket, is of dark blue material and is decorated with a great deal of embroidery. It has two very interesting features. One is the heavily embroidered white linen shoulder pieces that look like epaulettes. The other is the group of red wool pompons fastened to the front. Two large pompons are affixed to the collar, one on each side, and two smaller ones are fastened to the lower part. This exceptionally stunning garment can be made from a man's ordinary vest covered with blue material. The embroidery can be simulated by sewing on brightly colored pieces of figured crepe.

The Moravian hat is a small circular affair, made of black and red wool—black on the sides and red on top. It can be reproduced by sewing heavy black material around a circular cardboard framework and adding a top of red flannel.

The Moravian women's costume is as striking as that of the men. The skirt is of blue and reaches about half-way to the ankles. It is very full, being worn over two or three petticoats, each of which is trimmed with lace.

The skirt is completely covered in front and at the sides by the woman's most valued possession—the apron. These are usually heavily embroidered, but not always. One that can be easily reproduced has little or no embroidery and is very brilliant. It is of bright red material with widely spaced white flowers. A short distance from the bottom it is encircled by three bands of ribbon, colored green, yellow, and blue. These aprons are fastened with long brocaded ribbons that encircle the waist and are tied in front. The ends hang down in front as shown in the drawing.

The blouse is made of white cotton or linen. It is gathered at the neck and the neck is finished with a ruffle about three inches in width. The sleeves of the blouse are its most distinctive feature. They are very full and are gathered at the elbow as shown in the drawing. In a home-made costume, a circular piece of wire may be sewed inside the sleeves to give them the proper shape. At the elbows the sleeves terminate in bands of embroidery and large embroidered ruffles. On the upper part of each sleeve there is a wide band of red and blue embroidery.

Over the blouse is worn a sleeveless close-fitting jacket, or corselet, of dark blue. It is lavishly decorated with embroidery. To its front are attached two large red woolen tassels, or pompons.

The stockings worn with this costume may be either black or white, and the oxfords or slippers are black. Many of the Czechoslovakian women still wear the traditional soft leather knee boots such as those pictured; but copies of these are usually difficult to obtain, and the costume is quite authentic with shoes and stockings.

The head is covered by a cap or kerchief, several of which are illustrated. The kerchief is either tied at the back or knotted

CAP

KERCHIEF

MORAVIAN

CZECHOSLOVAKIA

beneath the chin. Some kerchiefs are white and edged with lace; others are of bright red and yellow material and resemble a bandana handkerchief.

## DENMARK

THE Danish costumes are easy to make and their effect is very delightful. There are minor variations in the costumes of the different Danish provinces but these are less marked than in many of the other countries, where people of totally different lineage have been included within the national boundaries. The costumes described may be considered, therefore, as typical of all of Denmark.

The man's breeches, which are not very full, button at the knee and can be reproduced with a pair of old golf trousers. The most common colors are brown, blue, and dark green. The woolen stockings may be dark colored, gray, or red, the color varying just as the color of golf stockings varies with us, according to individual taste. Woolen garters are tied around the stockings just below the knee. The shoes are black with large silver buckles.

The shirt is an ordinary soft white shirt and the necktie is a large flowing scarf tied in a double knot. Over the shirt is worn a short jacket fastened with a double row of buttons. It is usually made of the same kind of material as the knee-breeches. Instead of this arrangement, the man can wear a tunic with a band collar and a single row of buttons. Both are part of the old national costume.

The man wears an old-fashioned stocking cap which, like the stockings, may be of any color, or else a black felt hat with a very tall domed crown.

The woman's woolen skirt is full and comes down to the ankles. It is generally worn over two or three other woolen skirts, but these extra garments are not necessary for a costume. Favorite colors are blue and red with bands of a contrasting color such as yellow near the bottom. Over the skirt is a white apron with a band of multi-colored crosswise embroidery near the lower edge. The stockings are either white or colored and the slippers are black with silver buckles.

The white blouse may have either short or long sleeves. The waist is held in by a bodice of black velvet, tightly laced with red ribbons and decorated with six large silver buttons, three on each side. A small fringed shoulder shawl or kerchief is thrown over the hair, knotted beneath the chin. See page 5 for pattern of bodice.

DENMARK

# FRANCE

THE costumes worn by the men and women of Brittany are the best known and most distinctive of the French peasant costumes.

A Breton sailor's costume is one of the easiest of all to make, but is always effective. It consists simply of reddish colored trousers and a jumper of the same hue. Beneath the jumper there is usually worn a blue ring-neck jersey or sweater, and a blue beret completes the costume. Scores of sailors clad in these picturesque costumes can be seen any day on the waterfronts of the Breton fishing-towns.

The holiday costumes of the Breton peasants, are, of course, more elaborate than the fishermen's working-clothes. The men wear very full trousers, almost bloomers, that are gathered in at the knees. These are usually dark blue or black. A broad white belt encircles the waist. Black woolen stockings and black shoes with buckles or wooden sabots complete the lower part of the costume. It should be mentioned that the Breton men frequently wear stockings embroidered around the ankles. A note of authenticity can be given the costume by sewing part of a child's gayly-colored sock to an ordinary pair of black stockings at the ankles. Red and white stripes are a commonly used design.

The shirts worn by the Breton men generally have a high neckband, instead of an open collar. Over the shirt is worn a tight-fitting blue sleeveless woolen vest. The costume is completed by a dark blue, long-sleeved coat of the type shown in the illustration. It can be made from a pyjama jacket. The coats are almost always heavily embroidered in red and white in the front and on the collar and cuffs. This bit of color can be added by adding gayly-colored cloth or crepe paper. The typical Breton hat is of black felt and has a flat crown and a very broad brim. Around the crown runs a band of ribbon, usually dark in color, the ends of which hang down over the brim. These ribbons are sometimes only a few inches long, but frequently hang down as low as the waist.

The holiday costumes of the Breton women are generally much more brilliant and varied in color than are those of the men, who adhere chiefly to blue or black. The costume illustrated, with its cheery red and white, is indicative of this tendency.

The red skirt is full and long, and is heavily embroidered at the

BRETON

PEASANTS

BRETON
SAILOR

FRANCE

bottom. This embroidery can be reproduced by sewing bands of figured material or crepe paper to the skirt. Over the skirt is a gayly-colored apron, with a vivid flower design. These aprons are generally heirlooms and among the owner's most treasured possessions. White or red stockings and black shoes with silver buckles or wooden sabots are worn on the feet. The long-sleeved shirtwaist is white with a round collar. Sometimes a plain collar is worn; at other times it is embroidered. Over it is worn a bodice of figured material similar to that of which the apron is made. The bodice is edged with embroidery, or a strip of decorative material, and is cut to overlap as shown in the illustration. The costume is capped off by the simply-made white Breton cap. The pattern is shown on page 5.

## GERMANY

THROUGHOUT Germany the peasant dress consists of the same general garments, although there are, of course, many minor variations. The men wear knee-breeches or long fairly tight-fitting trousers, vests, and short jackets, while the women wear full, heavy cloth skirts, white or colored blouses, tightly-laced bodices, and neckerchiefs. It is chiefly in the women's headdresses that marked variations are found between different parts of the country. In southern Germany, the Tyrolean folk costume is very commonly worn.

The man's costume illustrated is one worn in northern Germany, but it is also typical of the country as a whole. The breeches are fairly tight-fitting and are fastened at the knee with two silver buttons. Golf knickerbockers may be used, or flannel pyjama trousers cut off short and gathered in at the knee. The stockings are either white or colored, as red or black. The shoes are of heavy black leather.

A soft white shirt is worn with a black silk cravat tied in a double knot with short ends. Over the shirt is the most distinctive part of the costume, a heavy red woolen vest or jumper. It is sleeveless and is decorated with two rows of large silver buttons. In some parts of Bavaria, coins are used instead of buttons. This garment can be made by using either a man's ordinary vest or a close-fitting pyjama top as a base.

BLACK
FOREST
HAT

TEGERNSEE
WOMAN

BAVARIAN
HAT

SCHLESWIG-
HOLSTEIN
HAT

# GERMANY

This costume, as has been said, is typical of all parts of Germany. The type of headdress worn will indicate which specific locality the wearer comes from. In Baden and Wurttemberg, the men wear a black felt hat with a low circular crown and a curled brim; while in Schleswig-Holstein a white stocking-cap is the customary headgear. Bavarians use the green "Alpine" hat trimmed with flowers or feathers; Prussians, of the Spreewald region, wear a simple cloth cap with a visor; and the men of Hessen fancy a small fur toque with a crown of green velvet.

The woman's costume illustrated is characteristic of the region surrounding the Tegernsee in southern Germany. The skirt is full and is made of striped material, red, blue, and black, being a common combination. If material of this kind is not available, dark blue is appropriate. Over the skirt is an apron that may be white, pink, or of figured material. Frequently the apron is edged with lace and has a lace insertion near the bottom. The stockings are white and are worn with black slippers.

The blouse is red or blue and its square-cut neck is edged with white lace. Its sleeves may be very short, reaching only half way to the elbow, or they may cover the entire arm to the wrist. An ordinary blouse with a square neck can be used, for very little of the blouse is seen, except for the sleeves and the lace around the neck. It is almost entirely covered by the black cloth or velvet bodice fastened at one side with hooks and eyes and is decorated in front with numerous small silver chains to which are fastened several large silver coins. The bodice is made from a single oblong piece of cloth, cut to fit snugly around the waist and fitted with hooks and eyes for fastening. In the top of the bodice in front are inserted several sprigs of flowers. These are distinctive Bavarian customs, not found elsewhere in Germany.

The kerchief may be white, pink, or figured material. It is of generous width and its ends are tucked out of sight beneath the bodice.

The women of Tegernsee wear a brown or green velour hat with a small crown and an upturned brim. This can be reproduced by a man's felt hat with a narrow curled brim. Invariably a feather ornament or a sprig of flowers is tucked into the band.

A second woman's hat is included which is worn in the Black Forest of southern Germany. The hat is an ordinary straw one, but it has seven or eight large velvet pompoms sewed to it in the manner shown in the drawing. If the pompoms are red they denote that the wearer is married, if black, that she is single. Beneath the hat is worn a circle of net or chiffon, the ribbon ties passing through it.

# GREECE

THE traditional men's costume of Greece is called the *fustanella*. It originated in Albania and until recently was the uniform of the king's guard. Instead of trousers, the fustanella has a wide billowy white skirt that reaches to just above the knees. This can be reproduced by using four or five pieces of pleated white crepe paper, one placed over the other. The legs are encased in long white leggings that are encircled just below the knee by red ribbon garters. Long white cotton stockings or long-legged underdrawers can be used for the leggings. The shoes are of black leather and have upturned points to which are fastened red pompons.

The shirt is white and, in the old costume, had wide sleeves that were loose at the wrists. If strict historical accuracy is not essential, an ordinary soft white shirt can be used, as this is the type worn by many of the young men of Greece today. The shirt is secured at the waist by a broad red sash, to which is attached the wearer's dagger in its broad leather sheath.

The high-necked vest is made of scarlet cloth and is fastened on the right-hand side with a row of about twelve round red, blue or silver buttons. It can be reproduced by using a man's vest as a foundation.

The customary headwear is a soft red stocking-cap with a tassel of blue silk.

The Grecian woman's costume illustrated is that worn in Epirus. It includes the long sleeveless coat that is the most characteristic article of apparel in the Greek peasant woman's dress.

The skirt, which reaches to just below the knee, is made of the favorite dark blue material decorated with gold embroidery. It is held in place at the waist by a broad gold-embroidered belt fastened by a large ornamental clasp. The stockings are white and are worn with black or red slippers.

The loose-fitting blouse is deep rose or plum-colored and is edged with gold braid at the neck and wrists. The sleeves flare out below the elbow and are slit on the inside for a distance of about six inches, as shown in the drawing.

Over the blouse is the long sleeveless coat. This is frequently of the same material as the skirt—in this instance, dark blue. It is edged with a two-inch band of gold braid on the outside of which is a

"PILL BOX" HAT

SLIPPER

BELT

# GREECE

looped edging, while the body of the coat is lavishly embroidered with golden thread. For costume purposes, the decoration need not be applied so generously. The shape of the coat alone will provide the authentic Greek touch to the costume, and a broad edging of yellow sateen will lend sufficient color.

The headdress is a little round white "pill box" hat to which is attached a blue fringed tassel. It can be made by sewing white cloth around a cardboard or buckram foundation.

# HAWAII

THE girdle, or *malo,* worn by the Hawaiian men and the grass *hula* skirts of the Hawaiian girls and women require but little description. The men's *malos* were originally of tapa cloth made from the bark of trees and brilliantly dyed. Today the men replace the tapa cloth with gaudily colored cottons.

For costume purposes, the man should wear a brown singlet on the upper part of his body. A *lei,* or a string of shells, may be worn around the neck and crepe paper flowers may peep from behind the ears.

In the olden days, both men and women sometimes wore a mantle made of long grasses, such as the one pictured. This can be made of strips of brown and yellow crepe paper sewed to a tape that encircles the wearer's neck.

The woman wears a brown bodice and an imitation grass skirt made of strips of brown and yellow crepe paper sewed to a knee-length brown cloth foundation.

Leii, or flower garlands, can be made from red or yellow crepe paper. Cut a long strip of paper about 1½ inches wide. Gather it lengthwise through the middle with needle and thread. Then twist the paper around and around the thread until it forms a series of circles.

For footwear, if you need it, use beach sandals or slippers.

MANTLE

HAWAII

# HOLLAND

THE Dutch costumes with which we are most familiar and which can most accurately be described as typical are those worn by the inhabitants of Volendam and Marken, on the Zuyder Zee.

The men of Volendam wear the wide, full Dutch trousers that are pleated at the waistband and ornamented with two large silver buttons. The traditional color is dark blue, though red is also used. For footwear, the Hollander does not always wear his wooden sabots, or *klompen*. These are frequently replaced by soft black leather slippers which, to say the least, are easier to wear at a party or in a play than the sabots.

The Volendammer's shirt is of red and white striped baize. It can be reproduced by using a finely striped man's shirt. Around the neck is a red kerchief that is folded as shown in the drawing, instead of being knotted.

Over the shirt is a tight-fitting jacket, or *blempie*, which in color is either dark blue or red. Important adjuncts of the *blempie* are the silver buttons worn on the right side of the neck and the short silver chain on the opposite side. This garment can be reproduced by adding sleeves to a man's vest.

The Volendammer always wears on his head the tall fur *ruigie*. It can be reproduced by sewing black woolen cloth over a cardboard frame. When a man is engaged to be married, he pins three or four small green silk bows to his *ruigie*.

The men of Marken wear very full, dark gray breeches that come just below the knee, black woolen stockings, and sabots or slippers. The upper part of the body is encased in a tight-fitting double-breasted jacket of the same material as the breeches. In the summer they wear a broad-brimmed black felt hat and in the winter a close-fitting fur cap.

The Volendam women and girls have full skirts that are worn over from four to seven petticoats. In addition a roll of cloth is worn around the hips. The skirt is frequently of striped material, red, blue, and white, or it may be solid red or blue. Over the skirt is a thick, woolen, dark blue apron with a piece of flowered material at the waist. This is the traditional apron and is much worn, but plain white aprons are also used. The apron covers the sides of the dress as well as the front. White or black stockings are worn with sabots or black slippers.

VOLENDAM

MARKEN

HOLLAND

On the upper part of the body is worn a close-fitting dark blue bodice, or *kledje*. This has elbow-length sleeves and reaches to below the waist, its lower portion being covered by the apron. It has a square, low-cut neck, beneath which there is a piece of brightly-colored flowered cloth. A pleated white kerchief is worn around the neck, its ends being tucked beneath the front of the bodice.

The headdress of the Volendam women is the well-known *hulletje,* a white cap with wings at the side. This can be fashioned from white cambric or crepe paper. The pattern is shown on page 5.

The women of Marken wear dark blue or brown woolen skirts that are held out at the sides and back by a bustle. Over the skirt is a gaily colored apron of checked or figured material. A red and white check is good for costume purposes. *Klompen* are worn out-of-doors; square-toed black leather shoes with silver buckles indoors.

Marken bodices are always very gay. They are made of flowered or striped material, lace in the back, and have straight sleeves that reach midway between wrist and elbow. Frequently the sleeves are of a different material than that of the bodice itself. A favorite combination is the one illustrated. The front of the bodice is white in the center and is flanked by two strips of checked or striped material, while the sleeves are of flowered material.

The cylindrical hat worn by the Marken women is a work of art. It is composed of three white muslin caps, or bonnets, placed one above the other around a cardboard shape. It is held together by three red and two black ribbons. This headdress is removed only once a week for freshening up. The wearer not only carries it during the day all the rest of the week, but sleeps with it on at night. It can be reproduced by sewing white muslin around a cylindrical cardboard foundation.


# HUNGARY

THERE are a number of unusual features about the Hungarian costumes that make them of great interest. Nothing quite like them is found in any other part of Europe.

The most striking part of the man's costume is the white linen *gatyak,* or trousers, that are so wide they resemble a divided riding skirt. They can be reproduced most easily by making an actual skirt. The final appearance will be almost exactly the same as if two separate skirt-like trouser legs were made. The extreme width

SZUR

GATYAK

HUNGARY

of this garment may be realized from the fact that the wearer can lift the hem of either leg out level with his shoulder.

A heavy leather belt ornamented with numerous brass circles is worn around the waist.

The Hungarian men wear either heelless leather shoes that are very similar to Indian moccasins or, more commonly, black leather top-boots. For costume purposes, riding boots may be worn or imitation boots may be made from black oilskin.

Almost as unusual as the *gatyak* are the sleeves of the white linen shirt. These are very wide and reach about six inches beyond the finger-tips. The shirt is embroidered in black and red, or black and white, on the collar, in front, and at the cuffs of the sleeves. This embroidery may be reproduced by using figured cloth or crepe paper. It is an essential part of the costume and should by no means be omitted.

The hat is a small round black, or dark green, felt with a small upcurved brim. It is invariably decorated with sprigs of flowers or stalks of grass. A child's hat can be used to represent this headgear.

The most interesting garment of all, perhaps, is the Hungarian *szur,* or long coat of white felt. The best way to reproduce it, without making an entire garment, is to use a woman's long white coat and decorate it with cloth or crepe paper. The original is long and has wide, straight sleeves, broad lapels, and a square-cut sailor collar. It is fastened in the front by two leather straps that buckle over the chest. The Hungarian man never puts his arms in the sleeves, but hangs the *szur* over his shoulders as though it were a cape. The garment is decorated with broad red and black bands and embroidery or appliqué. The drawing shows a characteristic decorative pattern.

Many of the Hungarian peasant women's costumes and head-dresses are so elaborate that it would be impossible to reproduce them without an infinite amount of painstaking work. For that reason, one of the simpler costumes that is common to nearly every section of the country has been selected for illustration.

The skirt is full and reaches to the ankles. Commonly worn colors are dark blue, purple, and lavender. Over the skirt is an apron of white, pink, red, or blue, that is generally quite plain. The stockings are either black or white and are worn with black slippers.

The white, or colored, shirtwaist is usually quite plain, but has a narrow standing collar. The sleeves are either elbow length or reach to the wrist. Most of the shirtwaist is hidden beneath a brilliant embroidered and fringed shawl, the ends of which are crossed in front and fastened at the waist by a large brooch.

The head is covered with a brightly colored scarf bound around the forehead and tied in the back.

## INDIA

THE Indian man's costume with which people in the West are most familiar is that worn by the Mohammedans. Its narrow white trousers, somewhat resembling jodhpurs, are different from those worn with any Occidental costume. The Hindus of India generally wear a *dhoti* instead of trousers, this being a long strip of white cotton cloth that is wound around the hips, the ends being passed backwards between the legs and tucked in at the waist.

The Mohammedan man's ankle-length white trousers are called *pa'ejamas,* and are the ancestors of our modern-day pyjamas. They are generally close-fitting and cut on straight lines, though sometimes they are cut very full about the waist and knees and taper from the knees down. A pair of pyjama trousers will reproduce them. If the very close-fitting effect is desired, some of the material can be removed from each leg.

The upper part of the body, as well as the greater part of the trousers, is covered by a long white, or colored, cotton coat, the *anga.* This has long, wide sleeves and a round or narrow standing collar. The coat itself buttons up the front and is fastened with a narrow belt, or sometimes a broad, brightly-colored sash, at the waist. While white is the customary color, red, blue and green are sometimes used and these colors are suggested for a play or party costume because of their more brilliant effect. The *anga* can be reproduced by remodeling an old-fashioned night shirt or by adding a skirt to a pyjama top.

The natives of India wear either red leather shoes with upturned toes or sandals of a number of different varieties. Low-heeled red morocco bedroom slippers are a good substitute for the shoes.

The head covering is generally either a turban or a tarbush, which is similar to a Turkish fez but has no tassel. The turban is made of a strip of fine cotton, measuring from ten to fifty yards long. It is wound around the head in various ways, with one end always hanging down the back.

The Indian girl's or woman's costume illustrated is more typical of that worn by the Hindu women than by the Mohammedan. The latter favor trousers like those worn by the men instead of skirts.

The skirt of the costume illustrated is of scarlet decorated with a band of gold embroidery at the bottom. The upper part of the body is clad only in a tight-fitting white or colored cotton blouse, the *cholee,* so short that it does not quite reach the top of the skirt. It has a V-neck and short sleeves that just cover the elbow.

The most important part of the costume is the beautiful scarf, or *sari,* that is draped around the head and shoulders. This is made of fine cotton or silk and is always marvelously colored. It is draped over the head and shoulders, one end falling almost to the ground on the left side, the other end being brought up over the left shoulder.

On her feet the Indian woman wears red leather slippers or sandals, similar to those used by the men, and jeweled anklets.

The drawings also show the costumes worn by a native maharajah and his wife, or ranee, of Rajputana. The man wears long, narrow white trousers gathered in at the ankles. These can be reproduced with white pyjama trousers. For the rest, he is clad in a richly embroidered robe which has a round neck and is girded in at the waist by a broad sash. This can best be imitated by using a silk dressing gown trimmed with plenty of gold braid. Several necklaces encircle the maharajah's neck and on his head he wears a tall turban of red cloth bound with a golden band. This can be made by wrapping red canton flannel around a buckram foundation and securing it with a strip of gold or yellow material.

The ranee wears a close-fitting long-sleeved jacket that comes to the waist. The best way to imitate it is to use an ordinary round-necked, brightly-colored blouse or pyjama top. The rest of her costume consists of narrow ankle-length trousers, and the *sari* which is draped around her body as shown. Her headdress can be made from a rectangular piece of blue silk held in place, for costume purposes, by small strings fastened beneath the chin. A number of silver ornaments should be attached to it, if they can be obtained. Otherwise it should be decorated with gold and silver braid.

MAHARAJAH
AND
RANEE

HINDU
WOMAN

MOHAMMEDAN
MAN

INDIA

# IRELAND

THE old folk costume of Ireland has not been worn for many years, but its general characteristics are well known.

In the man's costume the tight-fitting light brown knee-breeches can be made from a pair of khaki Boy Scout breeches. The most popular color is light brown or buff, but black is also worn. The breeches are buttoned at the side of the knee. The woolen stockings are black and the thick-soled shoes, or "clogs," are of black leather.

The waistcoat, with its double row of buttons, is made of green material. It can be reproduced by covering a man's ordinary vest with cloth or crepe paper and sewing on the extra row of buttons.

A white soft-collar shirt is worn with a loosely knotted green or black tie, the ends of which need not be tucked inside the vest. No Irishman favors too great an amount of restraint in matters of dress.

The flowing tail-coat is of dark brown material. It can be made by sewing tails to an ordinary suit coat. A better plan, however, is to get a pattern for a Colonial man's fancy dress costume and make the coat by following it. These patterns are obtainable at most department stores.

The Irishman's hat, which completes the costume, is brown with a green band. It can be reproduced by affixing to an old derby hat, a cardboard crown cut to the shape shown in the drawing. If the derby is a black one, its brim can be covered with brown cloth or crepe paper.

Perhaps the most distinctive feature of the Irish girl's costume is that it includes two skirts. These are of wool or cotton. The underneath skirt is green and the outside skirt is brown or red. The latter is gathered up and pinned to itself. This is done to keep it clear of the ground while working in the garden or feeding the pigs. The stockings are white, red, or black. Either oxfords or slippers may be worn.

The shirtwaist is a plain white one without a collar. Around the waist is worn a small red or black bodice laced tight with green or red ribbons. (See page 5 for pattern guide.) The costume is completed by the green shawl, either plain or of plaid, the ends of which are tucked into the bodice.

SHAWL

BOY'S
JACKET

# IRELAND

# ITALY

IN ITALY, as in most of the other countries of Europe, the old peasant costumes are seldom seen today. It is said that when tourists first visited Italy in large numbers they made so great a fuss over the colorful clothes worn by the natives that the latter stopped wearing their traditional costumes, in order to escape the attention of the tourists. The costumes illustrated are typical of southern Italy and Sardinia, where the peasants have retained their picturesque dress to a greater extent than in other regions.

The man wears white baggy breeches that are buttoned at the knee. The stockings are white, red, or black. In southern Italy, it may be noted, reds of all shades are the most popular colors. The shoes are of black, hand-sewn leather, and may be adorned with silver buckles.

The blouse may be reproduced by using a man's soft white shirt. Over it is worn a red or brown sleeveless jacket with a double row of gilt buttons. A loosely knotted bandana handkerchief is worn around the neck, and a striped red and yellow sash is tied around the waist.

Over the left shoulder is carried a folded blanket, of red and yellow material. This is an essential part of the original costume, since many of those who wear it are herdsmen who are out in every kind of weather. Two types of headdress are illustrated, both of which are typical. One is a red stocking-cap, and the other a brown low-crowned, broad-brimmed felt hat with a red ribbon for a band.

The girl or woman wears a rather short full-cut skirt. It may be red, yellow, or blue. A broad band of contrasting material is sewed to it a few inches from the bottom. Over the skirt is a medium-long fringed apron, which is gathered in at the waist and fastened with ribbons. Frequently the apron is of dark material, blue, black, gray, or purple. In the original costumes, their lower parts are almost invariably richly embroidered. There is another type of apron worn in practically every part of Italy that is markedly different from the apron worn in other countries. It may be used to give a distinctively Italian touch to the costume. It is made of a strip of wool or silk, both ends of which are covered with embroidery. It is fastened over the skirt with a ribbon, and about a foot of its upper end is turned down at the waist.

**SCARF**

**HAIR
ORNAMENT**

**STOCKING
CAP**

**ITALY**

The stockings are white and the slippers are black with red pompoms.

The blouse is white with three-quarter length sleeves and a round neck. It is covered with a tight-fitting corselet fitted with two broad shoulder straps. This may be made of any brightly-colored material, either matching the skirt or contrasting with it. A red kerchief encircles the neck and shoulders.

The woman's headdress may be made of white cheese-cloth. This is sewed around a stiff cardboard form of the shape shown in the drawing. In the back, the headdress hangs down as far as the waist. If one does not wish to make the headdress, a red, yellow, or blue scarf thrown over the hair and knotted in the back, may be used instead.

## JAPAN

MANY Japanese are today discarding the ancient folk dress of their country for the less picturesque clothes of the Occident. In the interior, however, the traditional kimonos, obis, and other articles of apparel are still worn. These are the costumes to use for "The Mikado" and other Japanese plays.

Traditionally, the Japanese man wears a dark ankle-length kimono of blue, dark gray, or black. It is practically the same as the kimono worn by the women, the principal difference being that the sleeves are shorter for the men. Simply made kimonos can be purchased so inexpensively in our stores today that for costume purposes, the wisest course is to buy one. If it is light in color, it can easily be dyed. The kimono is always worn with the left side lapped over the right.

Around his waist the Japanese man wears the wide sash, or *heko-obi*. It is wound around the waist two or three times and tied at the back in a loose bow-knot. Common colors for the obi are blue and black. On formal occasions, the *kaku-obi* is worn. This is practically the same as the *heko-obi,* but is of stiff silk and is tied in a double knot.

Over his kimono the man wears a black silk, wide-sleeved, knee-length coat, or *haori*. It is very similar to a short kimono and can be reproduced by cutting an inexpensive kimono down to the proper length and dyeing it black. It is not lapped over as is the kimono, but is fastened by two cords tied across the chest. The crest of the

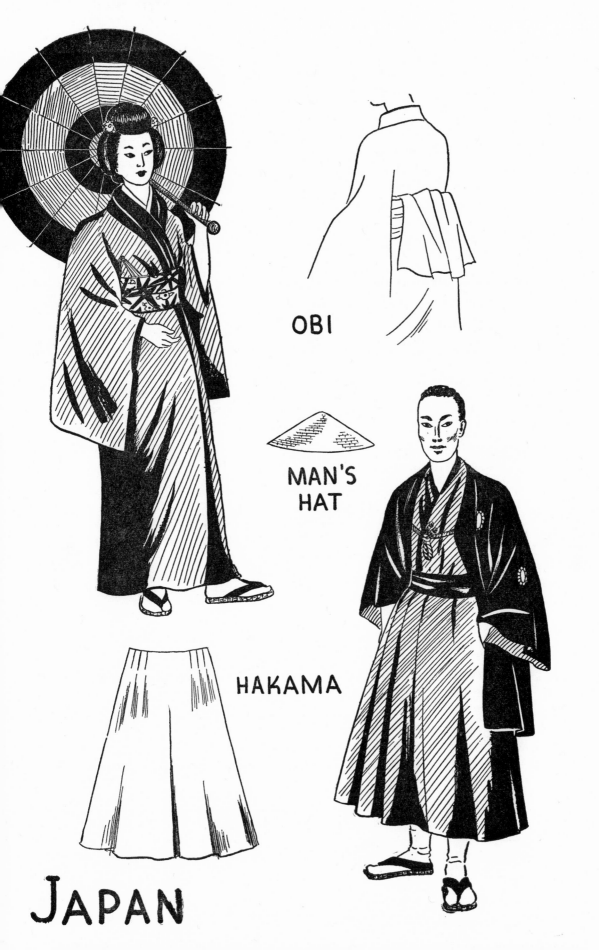

OBI

MAN'S
HAT

HAKAMA

JAPAN

wearer's family is stenciled or embroidered on both the *haori* and the kimono, in the center of the back, at the elbows of the sleeves, and on each side of the front at the level of the chest.

On formal occasions the man wears a pair of very full silk trousers, the *hakama,* that resembles a divided skirt. Their fulness is taken care of at the waist by pleats, of which there are six in front, three on each side, and two in the back. If these are included in the costume, they will have to be made, as there is no Western garment from which they can be adapted. Their appearance is clearly shown in the illustration and they are generally dark in color—blue, black, or gray—although pale yellow and green are also used. A stiff cloth belt is attached to the top of the *hakama.* Two cords are attached to the belt, one at each side in the front. These pass over the obi and are tied in back to hold the garment up.

Japanese stockings, or *tabi,* are white and are in reality socks, for they reach only to above the ankle. They have separate divisions for the great toes. This is to make room for the large cords of the sandals which pass between the first and second toes, cross at the instep, and fasten to the side of the heel. Ordinary sandals or shoes may be used, of course, if regulation Japanese ones are not available.

The Japanese man frequently goes hatless but carries a parasol to ward off the sun. When traveling, however, a basket-shaped straw hat is worn.

The Japanese woman's kimono is worn so it either touches, or just clears, the floor. It is held at the desired level by a cord or narrow sash of silk encircling the waist. The kimonos worn by young women of good families are of every imaginable color but always subdued and soft. It is only the geishas and actresses that wear the bright, garish colors. The married women generally wear quiet gray, blue, or brown kimonos. The linings of these garments are frequently made of brilliantly colored material.

The obi, or broad sash of brocade, is the most important part of the woman's costume. It is often more gayly colored than the kimonos and is decorated from end to end with embroidered flowers and other graceful designs. The obi measures four to six yards in length and from twelve to fifteen inches in width. When being put on, it is folded lengthwise, the two edges being turned upward. It is then wound twice around the waist and the two ends are tied at the back in a butterfly bow or, by matrons, in a complicated flat knot. The final effect of this knot is shown in one of the drawings and can easily be duplicated. The butterfly bow is worn only by unmarried girls and brides.

When out-of-doors, the Japanese woman wears a *haori,* or knee-length coat, similar to that worn by the man. Frequently it is gayly colored, particularly when worn by younger women. For a head covering, a scarf is wrapped around the head and tied under the chin. Frequently, however, the scarf is dispensed with and a parasol is carried instead.

The stockings and sandals worn by the women are identical with those worn by the men. A fan is, of course, an indispensable part of the costume. When not in use, the Japanese woman tucks it into the folds of the obi.

# JUGOSLAVIA

JUGOSLAVIA, or the Kingdom of the Serbs, Croats, and Slovenes, contains many races, each with a different national costume. In many respects these costumes resemble each other. Both men and women, for example, in numerous sections, wear jackets of the bolero type. In general, the women's skirts are long and full and are covered by an embroidered apron, while the men wear knee-breeches that are usually tight-fitting instead of the bloomer type.

The man's costume illustrated is the one worn in Bosnia. The breeches are black and are gathered in tightly at the knee. The stockings are white or embroidered and the shoes black.

The soft-collar white shirt is worn open at the neck. Over it is worn a dark blue bolero, edged with strips of red and gold material. For the sash wound around the waist, the most colorful possible material should be chosen. Green, red, yellow, and blue stripes are commonly used.

The man's round brimless hat is made of dark blue wool. It can be reproduced by sewing heavy cloth over a circular cardboard framework cut to fit the wearer's head.

The woman's costume illustrated is that worn in Dalmatia. The full skirt is either white or colored. It is covered with a richly embroidered apron which, in Dalmatia, is frequently made of felt. It may be reproduced by using a figured crepe. The stockings are white, and red or black slippers are worn.

The blouse is white with a circular neck, and long sleeves. The bolero, or jacket, is of red material and is edged with gold braid. (See pattern guide on page 5.) Around the waist is worn a broad colorful sash. The women of Dalmatia wear a number of different types of headdress, most of which include a flowing scarf. The one illustrated is widely used and consists of a small red "pill box" hat, covered with a white silk or cotton scarf. To the "pill box" are attached a number of gold coins, which serve as ornaments and also show that the wearer has a dowry to offer her prospective husband. For the same reason, Dalmatian girls frequently wear a necklace of heavy gold coins, and this can appropriately form part of a home-made costume. Buttons, or cardboard disks, covered with gold paint can be used to represent the coins.

APRON

STOCKING

JUGOSLAVIA

# MEXICO

MEXICAN folk dress has been influenced both by the Spanish conquerors and by the dress of the country's earlier rulers, the Aztecs.

The modern Mexican Indian man wears a white costume of coarse cotton cloth consisting of trousers, shirt, grass sandals and straw sombrero, together with the gaily striped *zarape* which is thrown over the shoulders. This is a descendant of the Aztec *timatli,* and is about four feet long and two feet wide. Ordinary white cotton duck trousers and a man's white shirt will form the basis of this costume. The *zarape* may be made from any piece of heavy striped material. The sombrero, with its peaked crown and enormous brim, is difficult to reproduce, though an imitation can be made from buckram sewed to a cloth foundation, or from cloth stretched over a wire frame.

The costume of the well-to-do Mexican man consists of tight-fitting trousers, black shoes, a white shirt, sash, long-sleeved bolero-type jacket, and a white or gray felt sombrero, banded with silver. The trousers and jacket should be of dark material, black or blue. Both are heavily trimmed with silver braid and silver buttons. The trousers may be made from a union suit, or a pair of flannel pyjama trousers gathered in at the ankle. The jacket can be made by sewing long sleeves to a blue or black vest and adding the trimmings. The sash may be red or blue. The sombrero can be made as described above.

The Puebla costume illustrated has become the national women's folk costume for virtually all of Mexico. The skirt is red and is lavishly decorated with large sequins. The bottom and top of the skirt may be of flowered or striped material. The skirt is frequently held up by two broad strips of the same material that pass over the shoulders. The blouse is of white cotton and has a square embroidered neck and short sleeves. Sometimes it is encircled at the waist by a red or blue silk sash. White stockings are worn with high-heeled black slippers.

The headdress may be a white scarf or a broad-brimmed straw sombrero. If the scarf is not worn over the head, it may be draped around the shoulders. One or two heavy necklaces are an almost indispensable part of the costume.

Mexican women of Spanish descent use the Spanish costume, as

RICH MAN

MEXICAN
INDIAN

# MEXICO

described in the section on Spain, when they "dress up." Ordinarily they wear the usual clothes of American women.

Folk costumes for Mexican children are the same as those described for adults.


# NORWAY

THE Norwegian country people have worn a distinctive national costume for many centuries. At present it is found only in the remote villages and hamlets in the mountains. Both the men's and women's costumes illustrated are from the Hardanger district in Norway, where the old costumes have persisted more than in other sections of the country.

The man wears tight-fitting dark blue breeches that come below the knee and are fastened with four silver buttons. They overlap the white woolen stockings. The latter are encircled by red woolen garters which are hidden beneath the breeches; except for the two ends which hang down over the stockings as shown. The shoes are of black leather with large silver buckles.

The shirt is white and has a small turned-down collar. For a costume, an ordinary soft white shirt can be used. Over the shirt is a high-necked green vest, ornamented with red stripes and red edging, and three rows of silver buttons. It can be made from a man's ordinary vest, or from a flannel pyjama top.

The jacket is collarless and is made of dark blue woolen cloth. It is worn open and is decorated on each side with a row of silver buttons. The hat is of black felt and has a high crown and a floppy brim. It is very similar to our own felt hats and an ordinary black felt can be used to reproduce it.

The women of Hardanger wear a full black woolen skirt reaching from the waist about half way to the ankle. Over the skirt is a large white apron decorated with a wide band of needlework above an equally broad hem. The stockings and shoes are black.

The Hardanger corselet is very distinctive. It is almost always made of red cloth and is edged with black, or yellow and black, braid. Two typical patterns are shown. Filling in the open part of the bodice is a strip of red cloth decorated with flowers worked in colored glass beads and edged at the top with a band of black velvet.

The bodice is worn over a white cotton blouse that has long, rather full sleeves and a small turned-down collar. Around the waist is a

NORWAY

belt two inches wide. This is made of knitted red yarn decorated with colored beads, or of black velvet ribbon, which is sometimes similarly decorated. The belts usually fasten in the front with a large silver buckle, but they are sometimes held tightly in place by means of invisible hooks and eyes.

The little girls wear the same costume as their mothers, but have knee-length skirts.

## POLAND

THE Polish peasant costumes are among the most colorful seen in European countries and a great deal of pleasure and satisfaction can be gained from a careful reproduction of them.

The brightest part of the men's costume, which is that worn in the region surrounding Zduny, is the trousers, which are bright red with inch-wide black stripes. These are tucked into black soft-leather knee boots. If genuine leather boots are not available, imitation ones can be made by encircling the legs with heavy black cloth, or oil-cloth. The cloth is held in place by straps passed beneath the shoes.

A soft white shirt is worn with a red necktie of which only a small area is visible, since the dark blue or black tunic is fastened very close around the neck. The tunic is worn both with sleeves and without. For a party costume, the sleeveless type is preferable, as it permits the contrasting white of the shirt to be seen. A row of large brass buttons fastens the tunic in the front. It can be made from a pyjama top, which should be gathered in slightly at the waist, so the skirts will flare out a trifle.

The Polish man's hat is a flat-crowned, narrow-brimmed black felt encircled by a gay red ribbon. It can be reproduced by cutting down the brim of an ordinary felt hat, or can be made by sewing black cloth over a cardboard framework.

The Polish woman's costume, typical of the region surrounding Lowicz, is a blaze of color from top to bottom. The short full woolen skirt is made of broad-striped material. The brighter and cruder the colors, the more typical it will be. Reds, pinks, blues, and greens, separated by strips of white, are characteristic.

Over the skirt is an equally gaudy apron. This may be of the same pattern as the skirt or may have an entirely different set of even brighter colors.

The stockings are white and are worn with black slippers.

TUNIC

POLAND

The blouse is white and has full sleeves that are either loose or close-fitting at the wrist. The front of the blouse is entirely covered with gay embroidery. This may be reproduced by means of a piece of figured crepe. Around the waist is a two-inch-wide belt of striped material—blue and white, yellow and black, or red and green.

Numerous necklaces constitute an extremely important part of every Polish girl's holiday costume. Five or six medium-long amber or coral necklaces are worn, and above them, fitting closely around the neck, are ten or twelve strings of imitation pearls.

The hair is entirely concealed beneath the folds of a large bright yellow kerchief knotted in the back.

The children wear the same brilliant festal costumes as the grown-ups.


## ROUMANIA

THE typical costume of the Roumanian men is not difficult to reproduce and has a distinctive character that is very pleasing. The close-fitting trousers are made of wool or linen. They can be reproduced by cutting out part of each leg of a pair of white flannel pyjama trousers.

The upper part of the man's body is covered by a white tunic that reaches nearly to the knees. It has a turned-down soft collar and buttons up the front. A good way to reproduce it is to sew a skirt onto an ordinary soft white shirt. The join will be covered by the red or black sash wrapped around the waist. In the original costume, the sash is a very broad leather belt.

On Sundays and holidays the Roumanian peasant dons his choicest garment, a richly embroidered black velvet vest. This can be reproduced by covering a man's vest with black velvet or satin and sewing on a collar and short lapels such as those shown in the drawing. The collar and lapels may be of red or green material. The embroidery can be represented by panels of gaudily figured material sewed to each side of the vest in the front.

The hat is of black or brown felt with a narrow turned-down brim. It is given a jaunty appearance by the cockade of flowers stuck into the band.

The Roumanian woman's skirt reaches to just above the ankles and is either dark blue or white. If it is blue, it is edged at the bottom with a band of red ribbon. Over the skirt is worn an apron

APRON

MARAMA

BELT

# ROUMANIA

of red cloth with two-inch vertical stripes of blue. This reaches to the bottom of the skirt. Instead of the apron, one may wear the characteristic Roumanian overskirt. This consists of a single piece of brilliantly embroidered material that is wrapped around the waist from left to right. It is impossible to describe the elaborate floral and geometric designs with which these garments are decorated. In general, they resemble the more exotic of the Oriental rugs.

The stockings are white and are worn with black slippers.

Roumanian women's blouses, made of linen or soft cotton, are round-necked and are usually heavily embroidered. Blue, red, black, and gold are the favorite colors for this ornamentation. The designs are almost always geometrical. They can be reproduced by sewing panels of figured material to the sleeves and the front of the blouse. The meeting place of blouse and skirt is covered by a broad sash which may be green, red, blue, or multi-colored.

A sleeveless jacket, or bolero, is worn and this, too, comes in an infinite variety of colors and designs. (For pattern guide see page 5.) Sometimes it is plain white or black, sometimes black with gold embroidery, sometimes blue with red and gold cross-stitching.

The Roumanian peasant woman covers her head with a kerchief knotted in the back or wears the national headdress, or *marama*. This consists of a long veil of white silk or cotton that is wound tightly around the head, with one end falling gracefully down the back. Very often this is embroidered and decorated with numerous sequins.


### RUSSIA

THE characteristic costume of the Russian man is well known and easily reproduced. Though it varies greatly in different parts of the country, the men's dress is much more uniform than that of the women.

The loose-fitting trousers are generally made of homespun or hand-blocked linen. For costume purposes, they may be made of flannel pyjama trousers dyed brown or orange. The trousers are tucked into high leather knee boots. If these are not obtainable, imitation boots may be made of heavy black cloth or oilcloth sewed to the trousers and held in place by straps passing beneath the shoes.

The long blouse, or tunic, is made of white linen or of some brightly colored cloth, such as blue, green, or red. It has a standing

KERCHIEF

WOMAN'S BOOT

MAN'S VEST

RUSSIA

collar and full sleeves. The collar and the cuffs of the sleeves are decorated with embroidery, as is also the bottom edge of the tunic. More embroidery is placed over the row of buttons that fasten the tunic on the left-hand side. A broad belt encircles the waist.

Frequently, when dressing up for Sunday, the Russian man wears a heavy woolen vest with a double row of brass buttons over his tunic. This garment buttons close around the neck and is a colorful addition to a home-made costume.

The woman's costume illustrated is one of the most distinctive of the Russian folk dresses. It is the traditional garb of the women in the Kaluga district, south of Moscow.

The skirt, or *sarafan,* is of red or blue cloth. In the original costume it is made of brocade and is richly embroidered. Around the bottom are eight one-inch stripes, alternately red and yellow. White stockings are worn with black, heelless slippers.

The round-necked blouse is of white cotton or linen. The sleeves are very distinctive. They are long and very full at the top, gradually decreasing in size from the elbow to the wrist. They are cut considerably longer than the arm and consequently have a good deal of extra material that hangs in folds over the forearm. From the shoulder to the elbow, the sleeves are generally embroidered, or are of red or other colored material.

Over the chest is fastened a long silk or muslin apron that hangs nearly to the bottom of the *sarafan.* It is usually gay in color—yellow, pink, or blue—and frequently is covered with a small geometrical design. It can be reproduced by using either plain or figured material.

Out-of-doors, the Russian woman wears a sleeveless and collarless knee-length coat, a favorite color for this garment being deep blue. This garment can be reproduced very easily.

The head may be covered with a brightly colored kerchief, or a copy of the characteristic Kaluga headdress shown in the drawing can be worn. Its crown is made by covering a cardboard or buckram framework with red cloth. A roll of red or yellow cloth is wrapped around the base of the crown and tied in a single knot at the back, the two ends hanging half way down to the waist.

# SCOTLAND

EVERYONE knows the kilts and tartan plaids of Scotland. The national costume has changed scarcely at all during the generations and it is, of course, worn today whenever there is a suitable occasion. Many people, when making a home-made costume, find it interesting to select the tartan of some particular clan. There are nearly a hundred different kinds, each belonging to a specific Highland clan. They are listed and illustrated in a number of books that are available at most libraries.

The man's pleated kilt is not difficult to make. Beneath it the Scotchman wears a pair of tight-fitting dark colored shorts, that resemble ordinary swimming trunks. The kilt is supported by a broad leather belt from which is suspended by a metal chain the *sporan,* without which no Scotch costume is complete. It is a large leather purse with silver mountings, which is covered with white sheep's wool. Two tassels of black wool are attached to it as ornaments.

The *sporan* can best be reproduced by using an old silver chatelaine bag. Around the bag is sewed a cloth cover to which are attached numerous pieces of white yarn. The two tassels of black yarn are stitched in place as shown in the drawing.

The stockings are of heavy wool and may be of the same pattern as the kilt or a plain color. The shoes are brown or black brogues.

An ordinary soft white shirt is worn and the necktie, which may be red or plaid, is either a four-in-hand, or a flowing bow tie.

The coat is short and is usually of dark colored material, black, blue, green, or brown. It is difficult to reproduce from any man's ordinary garment and, in most cases, the wisest course will be to make one entirely or obtain one from a costumer. A possible substitute is a short smoking-jacket. The coat is worn open and is frequently fastened in front with a small metal chain.

Over his left shoulder, the Scotsman carries a folded plaid shawl. This is fastened to the shoulder by a large ornamental brooch or clasp. It should be of the same pattern as the kilt.

There are two kinds of hats, the tam-o'shanter and the bonnet. Both kinds are available in the department stores, and it is best to purchase one ready made. The bonnet can be made, however, by sewing a band of the proper plaid around an Army overseas cap.

The Scotch girl or woman wears a warm woolen skirt and a tight-fitting bodice of the same material. Commonly used colors are dark brown and green. The shirtwaist is a simple white one gathered into a round neck. The stockings are white and are worn with black slippers.

The principal feature of the woman's costume is the fine plaid worsted shawl. This is three yards long and is worn in a very distinctive manner. It is placed over the head, and one end hangs down to the bottom of the skirt on the right-hand side. The shorter end falls over the left arm. In front, the folds of the shawl are held together by a large ornamental brooch.

BLOUSE

SHOES

BROOCH

BONNET

SPORAN

SOCKS

SCOTLAND

# SPAIN

THE Spanish peasant dress, particularly that worn by the men, still retains the sobriety of the sixteenth century. The drawing shows a costume typical of that worn by the men of Aragon, which is one that has come to be widely recognized as characteristically Spanish.

The tight-fitting knee-length breeches are made of black velvet and are slashed at the knee, the slashes being fastened with long black ribbons. The stockings are white and the common footgear consists of hempen sandals or *alpargatas*. Bathing sandals of this type can nowadays be purchased in most department stores.

The shirt can be a man's ordinary soft white shirt. It is worn buttoned at the neck without a necktie. The short jacket is made of black velvet and has two rows of silver buttons.

The only bright colors in the costume are the broad silk sash, or *faja,* and the kerchief wound around the head. These are usually red, or red and yellow.

The Spanish peasant woman's costume is generally much gayer than that of the men. The costume illustrated is, like that of the man, typical of Aragon. The brightly-colored skirt is short and full. It may be red, black, blue, or green, while the bands at the bottom may be of any contrasting color. Over the skirt is a short straight apron. If the skirt is red, the apron may be black; but if the skirt is black, the apron should be of a brighter color. Multi-colored stripes are frequently used. The stockings are white and are worn with black slippers.

The short-sleeved blouse is of white cotton. It is almost entirely covered by the bright shawl, which is an indispensable part of every Spanish peasant woman's costume. It is of silk or cotton and usually has long fringed ends.

The typical Spanish headdress is, of course, the mantilla. This is a scarf made of black or white lace that is worn gracefully draped over a large comb. In the front the mantilla comes down to the edge of the forehead, while in the back it reaches as far as the waist. While the mantilla is worn continually by many women of the upper classes, the peasants wear it only on feast days. At other times, the peasant women wear kerchiefs thrown over the hair and knotted beneath the chin.

KERCHIEF

COMB

SENORITA

MAN'S
HAT

SPAIN

# SWEDEN

SWEDISH peasant costumes are gayly-colored and distinctive. There are literally hundreds of minor variations of the general type, for in Sweden each village has zealously perpetuated its local dress down through the centuries. The costumes illustrated have been selected as representative of the outstanding features of Swedish peasant dress.

The man's costume illustrated is that worn by the men and boys of Halsingland, in the north of Sweden. The knee breeches are made of dark blue or black woolen cloth and the woolen stockings are also blue or black. Just below each knee is tied a red woolen garter which ends in large fringed tassels.

A white shirt is worn, and over it a red woolen vest with a row of gilt buttons up the front. This vest can be made with a man's ordinary vest as a foundation. It is covered with red cloth or crepe paper and the neck is made smaller, so the top button will be almost at the wearer's throat. Over the shirt and vest is the typical long Swedish coat with small turn-up collar and gilt buttons. A reasonable imitation of this type of coat can be made by sewing extra material to the bottom of a pyjama jacket having a stand-up collar. For costume purposes, it can be eliminated altogether, as it is only worn in winter, and the men commonly go about at other times without it. On his head the peasant of Halsingland wears a red stocking-cap. This can be made of crepe paper, if a real cap is not available.

One of the most beautiful of the traditional women's costumes is that worn in Dalecarlia. In its principal features it is typical of the costumes in other parts of the country. The most colorful part of the costume is the red, black, and white striped apron. If striped cloth is not available, this can be made from crepe paper. Under the apron is worn a long, full dark blue or red skirt. The white shirt-waist is made of cotton cloth and has a turned-down collar which is frequently made of brightly-colored material. Sometimes the shirt-waist is open at the neck and a gay kerchief fastened with a brooch takes the place of the collar. It has long sleeves that are fastened with buttons at the wrist. Short sleeves are not used in Sweden because the summers are short and cool.

Over the shirtwaist is worn a tight-fitting bodice, made of black or red material. (See pattern guide on page 5.) To it are attached two shoulder straps. The Dalecarlian women wear white

KERCHIEF

MAN'S
VEST

SWEDEN

pointed caps like the one illustrated. Sometimes these are plain and sometimes they are edged with lace. Stockings are usually white, though red stockings are commonly worn by girls and women in many parts of Sweden and can be used if the color they add to the costume is desired.

## SWITZERLAND

THE most widely-known of the native costumes worn by the men of Switzerland is the so-called "Alpine" or mountaineer's costume, which is the same as that worn in the Austrian Tyrol. This costume is described in the section devoted to Austria. There is no other Swiss peasant man's costume that has become well known or that could be considered typical. Therefore, in costuming a play about Switzerland, such as "Heidi," clothe the men and boys in the Austrian Tyrolean costume which is worn in both countries.

The Swiss woman's or girl's costume that has been selected as the most typical is the one worn in the Canton of Appenzell. The skirt is bell-shaped and is of blue, red, brown or black material with a broad red band near the bottom. It should be very full—from two to three yards in width. If desired, it can be made throughout of striped material, with blue and red predominating. Over the skirt is worn a short square-cut white apron. Sometimes this is made of lace. In a home-made costume, it can be made of white cotton cloth, or even of white crepe paper.

The white blouse, or chemise, has full sleeves ending in frills at the elbow, and a round neck encircled by a broad ruffle. This type of blouse is worn in all the Swiss cantons.

The tight-fitting corselet is made of black velvet and is laced together with red ribbons. (See pattern guide on page 5.) Beneath the lacing is a piece of pleated or gathered silk. This may be reproduced by using a piece of red or blue crepe paper.

The stockings are white. A typical Appenzell headdress is shown in one of the drawings. It consists of a small white cap to which are attached two wide pleated "wings." These can be made of white crepe paper, or of cloth supported by wire spreaders.

The little girl on the opposite page shows the correct costume for "Heidi."

SUSPENDERS
AND
BELT

SWITZERLAND

# TURKEY

THE Turkish man's costume is distinguished chiefly by its wide blue or red pantaloons, sometimes almost bloomers, and its red *fez* with a long blue tassel. The narrower type of pantaloon that was worn by ordinary citizens until Western dress was adopted after the war, can be made from flannel pyjama trousers dyed red or blue and gathered in at the ankles. Red leather slippers are worn.

The upper part of the costume consists of a white linen shirt which is almost entirely concealed beneath a high-necked vest of gay figured material. Over the vest is worn a long-sleeved blue, black or red bolero jacket. (For pattern guide see page 5.)

The Turkish woman wears full ankle-length trousers, or bloomers of red or white silk (use full pyjama trousers), heelless red or yellow slippers, a chemise of white silk, and a long coat, called a *yelek*. This garment is tight-fitting above the waist and buttons from the bosom to below the waist, but is open on each side from the hip downward. While typical, the *yelek* is somewhat difficult to make and may be dispensed with for ordinary costumes. Instead of it, a white or colored fringed scarf or shawl may be worn wrapped around the head, back and shoulders as shown in the drawing.

The old-fashioned headdress, or *yashmak*, is also useful for costume purposes. It consists of two squares of white or colored silk, each folded diagonally, and arranged over a small cap. One piece is placed over the head with the bias fold well down over the forehead, and pinned at the back. The second square is pinned in the same way at the back, but covers the lower part of the face so only the eyes and nose are visible.

The costume of a Turkish pasha of former times is illustrated for use in connection with Arabian Nights and other Oriental plays in which there is a Sultan and nobles of the court. His costume is, of course, of rich silks and brocades, which can be imitated by rayon, glazed cambric and cretonne.

A heavy silk dressing gown of blue or dark red would be excellent for the long robe that forms the pasha's principal garment. If this is not available, the robe can be made quite easily, as it has simple lines. It is girded at the waist by a broad sash of red, blue or gold. The outer garment—a flowing short-sleeved coat of yellow or blue brocade—will have to be made, unless one has an old bath gown from which the greater part of each sleeve could be removed.

PASHA

TURKEY

The most imposing part of the costume is the towering white and gold turban. This is best made from a large ball of tissue paper around which is sewed white rayon. Gold braid and feathers are added to complete it.

Arabian Nights princesses and dancing girls wear a costume quite similar to that of the ordinary Turkish woman. The garments should be shimmery, however, and made of rayon, silk or glazed cambric. Long delicately tinted scarfs are worn over the head and flowing down over the shoulders. Bracelets, necklaces and earrings are an indispensable part of the costume.

## WALES

THE old national costume of Wales is seldom seen today, except at the great song festivals such as the Eisteddfod.

The costume of the men consisted of brown or gray tight-fitting knee-breeches, a high-necked vest, over a white shirt, and a simply-cut dark-colored tail-coat. White or gray woolen stockings and heavy black leather shoes covered the legs and feet, and the head-gear was a low-crowned, broad-brimmed black felt hat.

The knee-breeches can be made from flannel pyjama trousers or tight-fitting golf knickerbockers. The vest can be adapted from a man's ordinary vest by adding extra material at the top. A little note of color was sometimes introduced by the vest, which was frequently of striped material. For costume purposes, narrow green and red stripes would be effective. The tail-coat is best made by following a pattern which can be obtained at a department store. It may be brown, plum, or gray in color. The shirt may be an ordinary soft white shirt, and the necktie is a narrow white ribbon tied in a loose bow.

The Welsh woman wears a full skirt, usually of black or black and white striped flannel. Over this is a long apron. This may be made of red cloth with figured bands across the bottom or of material with vertical stripes of red and white. Stockings are either white or black and the shoes are heavy brogues or slippers.

The shirtwaist is white and has three-quarter length sleeves ending in lace frills. A woolen shawl is worn about the neck and shoulders. It is folded so as to come to a point in the back.

WALES

The most individual part of the woman's costume is the hat. It is made of black glossy beaver, like a man's silk hat, but is shaped like a Hallowe'en witch's hat. The easiest way to reproduce it is to buy one of these witches' hats at the ten-cent store. Beneath the hat the Welsh woman or girl invariably wears a close-fitting white crocheted hood, somewhat like a baby's cap. Sometimes these hoods are plain, and sometimes they have large frills around the edge.

The hood is tied with a big bow beneath the chin. It can most easily be reproduced by fixing up a lace boudoir cap as shown in the drawing.

# PART II

# HISTORIC COSTUMES

# ANCIENT EGYPT

THE garments worn by the ancient Egyptians were quite simple and are not difficult to reproduce. The men of the higher classes and the nobles were quite content with a skirt, collar, and head covering of the types illustrated. The skirt is made of white or striped material. Stripes are more picturesque and may be of any combination of colors, for the Egyptians had many dyes. The most favored colors were yellow, green, red, light blue, tan and black. A straight piece of cloth of contrasting color hangs down between the folds of the skirt.

The wide, circular collar and the head covering are made from striped material. Some of these were made of woven material and some of beads. Armlets, wristlets, and anklets bearing the same design as the collar were frequently worn. The head covering is made of an oblong piece of material, one end of which is gathered in to fit closely over the head. Two tabs are then sewed onto the sides. Sandals are the proper footwear.

The king wears a skirt similar to that of the noble, but in front of it is fastened the king's apron. This is supported by a narrow girdle and is made from several pieces of figured and solid color cloth. The upper part of the body is partly covered by a light tunic and a wide collar rests on the shoulders. Sandals are worn.

The king wore either a headdress of the type illustrated, or the crown of upper or lower Egypt, both of which are shown. These are made from buckram covered with gilt paper or orange cloth to represent gold.

Egyptian slaves wore a simple white loin cloth.

The well-to-do or noble woman of ancient Egypt wore a simple white tunic, a long mantle, and a circular collar similar to that worn by the men. The tunic can be made from a plain white night gown. The mantle should be of some solid color such as red, blue, or green. It is made from a rectangular piece of cloth rounded at the end that is to be the bottom. Wristlets and anklets made of striped material should be worn and the feet should be protected by sandals. A band of brightly-colored ribbon encircles the hair.

The queen's costume consists of a white tunic, with a blue or red girdle, a short white cape fastened with a brooch in front, a wide decorated collar, and an elaborate headdress bearing the sacred vulture. Sandals are worn, and heavy silver bracelets instead of cloth

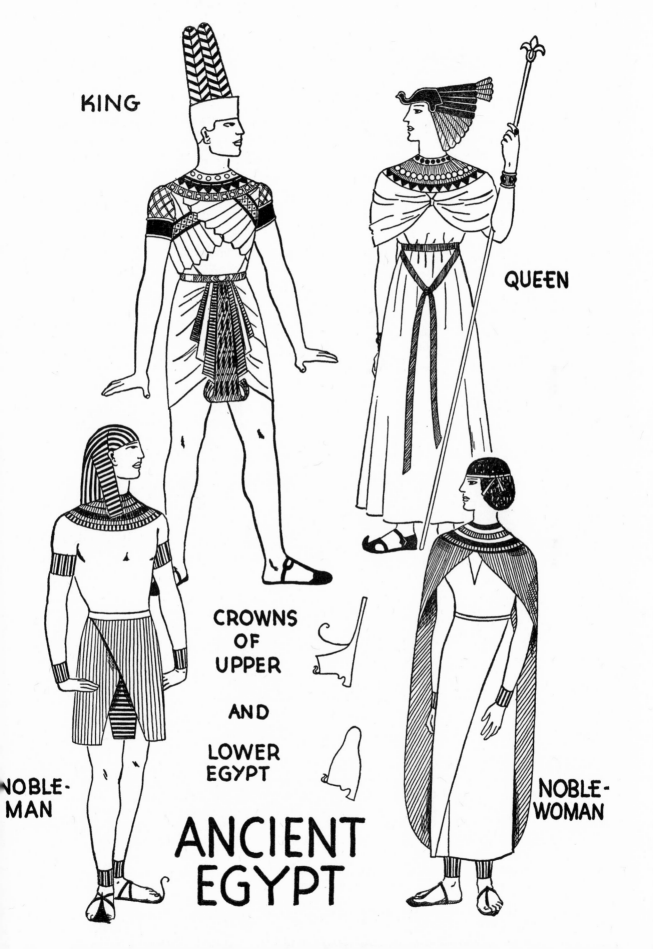

KING

QUEEN

CROWNS
OF
UPPER

AND

LOWER
EGYPT

NOBLE-
MAN

NOBLE-
WOMAN

# ANCIENT
EGYPT

wristlets. The headdress is made of buckram and cardboard covered with orange and black cloth. This costume is suitable for Cleopatra.

The slaves and women of the lower classes wore a long skirt fitted about the waist and supported by wide straps over the shoulders. This was either white or colored and was made of coarse flaxen material that can be best suggested by muslin.

## ANCIENT PALESTINE

THE men of Bible times and Bible lands wore either a short or long tunic over which was draped a voluminous, large-sleeved coat or a flowing mantle. For the costume of ordinary people or for the shepherds in a play dealing with the Nativity, the tunic is short and made of unbleached muslin. The coat is made of broad strips of sateen or gingham in deep colors—blue, orange, crimson, green and brown. The scarf used as a headdress may be white or of striped material and is encircled by two circular bands. These may be made from heavy cord or clothes line. For a merchant's or city-dweller's costume, substitute a turban for the scarf.

The pictures of Joseph and Mary on page 87 show the general features of the costumes worn in Bible lands.

The Wise Men, King Herod, and other people of rank or wealth, wear ankle-length tunics of striped material. The outer robe or cape is striped, or of a solid color and is girded at the waist with a richly-colored sash. Heavy sateen is a good material for the outer robe. King Herod's crown can be made from cardboard or buckram painted gold. Rich colors should be used for these costumes such as crimson, purple, orange and deep green. Sandals are worn.

The costume of the women was very simple, consisting chiefly of a simple one-piece dress with loose flowing sleeves and a scarf head-dress. The dress may be white with embroidery around the neck or may be of striped material such as that described in connection with the men's costume. It is held in at the waist by a colored girdle. The scarf is drawn around the forehead and pinned at the back of the neck, the remainder falling down the back.

Children's costumes were the same as those of their elders.

Useful books to supply greater detail and variety than can be given in the present volume are: "The Life of Christ as Represented in Art" by Dean Farrar, "The Life of Christ" by Tissot, "The Gospels in Art," edited by W. Shaw Sparrow, the "Peeps at Many Lands" series that is to be found in most children's libraries, and "The Primer of Production" issued by the Department of Religious Education of the Episcopal Church of America, 381 Fourth Avenue, New York City.

## ANCIENT GREECE AND ROME

THE principal garment of the men of ancient Greece was the *chiton,* or tunic, which was of the type shown in the drawing. This was made of linen or wool, which can be reproduced with muslin, woolen batiste, or cheese-cloth. A pattern for such a tunic is shown on page 5. The neck, sleeves and hem were generally decorated with borders of Grecian designs, several of which are shown. White was the usual color, though yellow, red, and blue were also used. The feet were clad in sandals.

Over the tunic was worn a *chlamys,* or mantle. This was a piece of white or colored material measuring about seven feet long and three and a half feet wide. It was thrown over the left shoulder and arm and its ends were fastened by a large brooch at the right shoulder.

The Greek woman's costume consisted chiefly of a long, sleeveless *chiton,* or tunic, of linen or wool, girded at the waist. The Greeks were fond of color and the tunic may be white, green, purple, crimson, blue, orange or yellow, and has a Grecian border round the hem.

There were two types of tunics, the Ionic and the Doric, both of which are illustrated. In its simplest form, the Ionic tunic consisted of two oblong pieces of linen twice the span of the arms in width. The ends are sewed together except for the arm holes and the top edges are held together by clasps or brooches. A girdle of ribbon encircles the waist and crosses the wearer's chest and back. With the Ionic tunic there was generally worn an over-garment that rested on the shoulders and fell gracefully down each side, its ends almost reaching the ground. It is made of two oblong pieces of cloth sewed together along one side except for the neck opening.

The Doric tunic is made from a single large piece of material draped around the body and fastened at the right shoulder and side. The top of the material is folded over to form a "bib" which reaches nearly to the waist. The tunic is held in at the waist by a girdle of ribbon.

Greek soldiers wore their armor over a tunic similar to that worn by the ordinary citizens. The armor, consisting of a corselet with an attached skirt of metal plates, and shoulder plates, can be made from buckram, oilcloth or canvas gilded or painted yellow. The leg guards are made from the same material as that chosen for the corselet. The helmet is made from buckram stitched to a cloth foundation, surmounted by a towering cockade made from red crepe

DORIC TUNIC

IONIC TUNIC

CHLAMYS

CHITON

# ANCIENT GREECE

paper. The shield is of beaver board and is painted in bright contrasting colors.

Roman boys wore a linen or woolen short tunic similar to that worn by the Greeks, while the men wore garments of the same type that reached to the ankles. Over the tunic was draped the toga. This was made of wool, linen, or silk, and was white for common citizens but purple for the emperor. The toga is semi-circular in shape and, measured from tip to tip, is three times the height of the wearer. To drape the toga properly, place one end at the left foot, carry the other end over the left shoulder, across the back, and under the right arm. Then bring the end across the chest and over the left shoulder, the remaining portion hanging down the back.

Men of the lower classes wore a hooded cloak of rough gray or brown material instead of the toga.

The Roman women and girls wore tunics similar to the Greek *chitons,* but without the Greek border designs. Frequently, however, they had a strip of solid color near the hem. Over the shoulders was draped the *palla,* a long oblong piece of material either white or colored. This was wound around the body in a number of different ways, one of the most common being shown in the illustration. Roman women often wore three or four tunics of different colors and of varying lengths, the topmost one being looped up at the waist to permit the others to be seen.

The Roman soldier's armor is made with strips of buckram, canvas or oilcloth painted with bronze or yellow paint. It is worn over a tunic of white or red cloth. The helmet is made of pieces of buckram gilded and stitched to a close-fitting yellow cloth foundation. Heavy sandals with leather thongs are worn.

Further illustrations of Greek costumes can be found in any illustrated history book and in "The Odyssey for Boys and Girls" by A. J. Church; "Greek Dress," by Ethel Abrahams, and "The Attic Theater," by Haigh. Good books for pictures of Roman costumes are "The Story of Rome," by MacGregor (in most children's libraries), "The History of France," by Guizot, and "Illustrations of Greek, Roman and Egyptian Costumes," by Baxter.

MAN
WEARING
TOGA

WOMAN
WEARING
PALLA

SOLDIER

# ANCIENT ROME

# MEDIEVAL EUROPE

*Crusader and His Lady*

THE chain mail armor illustrated is of the type worn almost universally throughout Europe from the eighth to the fifteenth centuries. It is the costume to use for King Arthur, Lancelot, or Ivanhoe. Plate armor did not come into general use until the middle of the fifteenth century.

A splendid foundation for the suit of chain mail is an ordinary union suit with socks sewed to the feet. Only the legs and arms need to be covered with imitation chain mail since the body is covered by the tunic or surcoat. The best way to reproduce the chain mail is to use the linked chain of which certain kinds of pot cleaners are made. These cleaners are obtainable at hardware stores, and some stores furnish large pieces of the same material. A suit made in this way is almost as realistic as an original garment. Another way to reproduce chain mail is to sew disks made of cardboard, heavy cloth, or tin, to the union suit foundation. If cardboard or cloth is used, the disks are given a coat of silver paint. Tin disks that are used for nailing down roofing paper are inexpensive and can be purchased at any hardware store. Still another method of imitating chain mail is to apply aluminum paint to net or very coarse canvas.

The sleeveless tunic is made of white cloth and has a large red cross stitched to it in the front. It is held in at the waist by a girdle made of red, blue, or black cloth, wrapped twice around the body and tied in the front.

The helmet is made of imitation chain mail sewed to a cloth foundation. Other appurtenances that may be included in the costume are a shield made of stout painted cardboard or beaverboard, a property sword, spurs, and a small cloth or leather purse. The custom of wearing a purse attached to the girdle was introduced by the Crusaders who called these receptacles *amonieres sarrasinoises,* or Saracen almsbags. Coins to give to the poor, and other small articles were carried in them. The fashion of wearing this small purse continued all through the Middle Ages, the women wearing them as well as the men.

The costume for a man of better class or a noble of this period, when not in armor, consisted of a long tunic, a flowing cloak, and

PEASANT

NOBLEMAN

EARLY MIDDLE AGES

CRUSADER IN CHAIN ARMOR

NOBLEWOMAN

soft leather pointed shoes. With a crown added, this costume is suitable for a medieval king. Patterns for both tunic and cloak are given on page 5.

The costume of the Crusaders' ladies was greatly influenced by the lines of their husbands' armor. The drawing shows the simplicity that characterized the dresses of the period.

The long one-piece dress or tunic is white and may be reproduced by using as a base a simple long white dress or nightgown. The pattern on page 5 may be followed if the tunic is made in its entirety. The neck is edged with colored material—blue, red, gold, or figured—and a narrow strip of the same material encircles the waist. The mantle is red or blue with a white lining and is edged with gold braid or figured material or crepe paper to simulate embroidery. This costume is correct for a medieval queen, such as Guinevere, or for Lady Macbeth.

### Peasant

Peasants of the early Middle Ages wore very simple garments. The man's costume consists of long close-fitting drawers or tights (use a union suit or flannel pyjama trousers) either plain or cross gartered with strips of brown cloth, a short tunic girded at the waist, and soft leather buskins. The latter can be reproduced with brown wool socks. The tunic can be made from a khaki shirt with long tails or by following the pattern for the Grecian tunic given on page 5. For peasant women, use a simple one-piece dress of the type worn by Maid Marian, described on page 92.

### Children

The children's costumes of the early Middle Ages are very much like those of their elders. The costumes shown in the accompanying illustrations can be used with slight variations, for noble and peasant children, throughout the whole Medieval Period from 600 to 1500 in England, France, Germany, Holland and Italy. They are also suitable for children characters in plays based on the fairy tales of Hans Christian Andersen and the brothers Grimm and for other fairy tale plays.

For peasant children the costumes should be made of cambric, muslin, tan poplin or serge.

For noble children the materials should be silk and satin. The noble boy does not wear the cloth around his shoulders, but simply a tunic. This could be of red or purple material trimmed with gold braid or imitation ermine. A tabard may be worn over the tunic. The girl's costume is made a trifle more elaborate by the addition of hanging sleeves. These were worn *only* by the nobility and the well-to-do people in medieval times, never by the peasants. The girl's costume may be of red, blue or purple with sleeves lined with white or some other contrasting color.

The costumes of the men, women and children are good for the "Pied Piper of Hamelin" and other medieval plays. The piper should wear a rakish hat with a long feather in it. The children's costumes can be used for "Hansel and Gretel," but a black laced bodice of traditional peasant type is often added to Gretel's costume and she is given a red or blue dress.

## Monk and Nun

The illustrations show the conventionalized costume worn by monks in the early years of the Christian era and in the Middle Ages. The costumes of the various orders differed from each other chiefly in the matter of color. Thus the Dominicans or "Black Friars" wore a long black mantle and hood, while the Franciscans were known as "Gray Friars" because of their coarse gray habit. The colors worn by the other orders can be found in any encyclopedia. The monk's costume consists of two garments, the long robe or mantle and the hood. It may be made from an old bath robe, or an inexpensive domino. If entirely home-made, use canton flannel, Turkish toweling or denim.

Friar Tuck, in Robin Hood plays, would wear this costume in brown, with the hood hanging down his back. If possible, a wig should be worn to reproduce the jolly friar's tonsured hair.

The nun's costume is a simple, flowing tunic of white, gray or black cotton material according to the order. It is girded at the waist, and a rosary on a long chain is attached to the girdle. The headdress is a wimple of white or of the same color as the tunic. The pattern for a long tunic given on page 5 can be used for both the monk's and the nun's costume.

In Morality or Mystery plays, the actors wear the costumes of the Middle Ages, not the costumes that were in use during New Testament days. This is because the Morality plays came into being during the Middle Ages and were originally given in medieval costume.

During the course of time, certain conventions came into existence in connection with the costumes of most of the characters that took part in the old Morality plays. To a large extent, these conventions were brought into being by the Craft Guilds in England which gave the plays year after year for centuries.

The Devil, for example, was always clad in black leather, wore a tattered mask, and carried a big club. Mary, the Mother, always wore deep rich blue, while Mary Magdalene was robed in scarlet. Judas was given red hair and a large red beard; King Herod always was clothed in a robe of blue satin and wore a helmet, and Joseph was clad in a simple dark gray or brown tunic without a headdress. The men saints wore a costume like Joseph's, and the women saints generally wore the straight gowns and semi-fitted sleeves of medieval times, together with the wimple or cowl-like headdress. The Christ was always robed in white and after the crucifixion, always wore a golden crown. Angels, in the old plays, had gold wings and skins.

The drawings give a very clear idea of the conventional Morality play costumes. All of them are easy to make and require little detailed description.

The Devil is a striking figure in black, with two red feathers on his head and scarlet facings on his sleeves. His hose are ordinary black tights or the drawers of a union suit dyed black. The doublet and close-fitting hood are made from black jersey cloth.

The Guardian or Militant Angel wears a one-piece mantle of golden cloth thrown over his left shoulder, and encircled by a broad golden belt. On his head he wears a circlet of stars and in his hand he carries a sword.

Other Angels wear simple white tunics of the types illustrated and have large gilt wings of cardboard or buckram.

Joseph, the Disciples, and men saints wore tunics of the kind illustrated, over which a one-piece sleeveless cloak of contrasting color may be draped. The cloak is made of an oblong piece of cloth about

MONK

NUN

JOSEPH

VIRGIN MARY

MILITANT ANGEL

DEVIL

MORALITY AND BIBLICAL

5 feet long. It is hung over the left shoulder, and the end hanging in back is carried diagonally across the back to the right hip. A stout cord holds it in at the waist.

King Herod is garbed as described under Ancient Palestine but wears a Roman helmet.

The Virgin Mary wears a white tunic with a golden girdle, a blue cloak, and a white veil bound around her head. When sainted, she wears the same costume, but with a crown.

Mary Magdalene has a one-piece dress of scarlet sateen, with a broad beaded girdle to which are attached strings of beads. The girdle may be made of buckram. Over her dress is a black one-piece sleeveless cloak or mantle. Her headdress is a scarlet kerchief, bound with strings of beads.


## THE LATE MIDDLE AGES
### 1300-1500

### Armored Knight and His Lady

A suit of plated armor such as the one illustrated can be made without very great difficulty by shaping the various parts from cardboard and buckram, and covering them with silver paper. Time and care are required for this task, but actually it is far easier to make a really satisfying suit of armor than most people imagine. The armor illustrated is of the type used in France and England in the fifteenth and sixteenth centuries.

A union suit is worn beneath the armor, as the backs of the legs and thighs are not covered by plate.

The breastplate and backplate are made from single large pieces of cardboard. The breastplate has a sharp crease in the front. Both pieces taper in sharply at the waist. Pieces of cardboard should be glued to the buckram to give extra strength and stiffness. Leave extra material at the sides of each piece, to make room for overlapping. When completed, punch overlapping holes in each side of both pieces. When donning the uniform, the breastplate and backplate are laced together with cord passed through the holes.

The lower part of the upper garment (*taces* and *tasset* in front; loin-guard in rear) are cut out of two pieces of buckram, one for the front and one for the back. They are also laced together at the sides when the armor is put on.

The *cuishes* that protect the thighs, and the *greaves* that cover the legs, are held in place by pieces of tape tied in the back. The tape is passed through holes punched for the purpose. The knee-caps are made from a child's leather knee-cap covered with silver paper. The "wings" attached to them on the outer side of each leg are cut from cardboard and are stitched or stapled to the knee-cap.

The feet are encased in socks covered with silver gray cloth. These are worn over low shoes.

The *fald* of chain mail is made in one of the ways described in the section devoted to the crusader and his armor.

The *pauldrons*, that protect the shoulders, and the *rerebraces* and *vambraces* that encircle the upper arms and forearms are made of buckram covered with silver paper. The *pauldrons* are held in place by tapes that pass beneath the armpits. The *rerebraces* and *vambraces* are simply slipped into place over the arms.

Leather knee-caps with cardboard "wings" attached are the best things to use for the elbow-cops.

The gauntlets can be reproduced by coating canvas gauntlets with silver paint, or a cuff made of buckram may be sewed on an ordinary glove and the whole given a coat of silver paint.

The helmet is made by covering a buckram foundation in the shape of a hood with silver gray cloth and stitching to it a silver-covered buckram vizor.

Like any other costume, a suit of armor is simply a combination of several more or less simply-shaped parts. When each part is regarded separately, it is seen that it can be cut and sewed to the proper shape with very little difficulty. When, however, the different parts are covered with silver paper and assembled, the completed suit is really magnificent.

When not encased in armor, the gentleman of the late Middle Ages (1300-1500) wore a costume consisting principally of long, tight hose and a doublet.

The hose were generally made of gay-colored silk and were sometimes each of a different color. Red, blue, purple, yellow—any rich solid colors may be used. The shoes were of soft leather or brocade.

The doublet, or tunic, was made of silk, satin, or velvet and was also richly colored. The long "dagged" oversleeve shown in the drawing was very popular, and was a unique feature of men's costumes during the late Middle Ages. An effective color combination is a purple doublet with yellow-lined sleeves, and yellow, crimson, or cloth of gold undersleeves. The belt may be of leather or may be of richly colored cloth that harmonizes with the rest of the costume.

The hose can be made from a union suit and the shoes reproduced by sewing cloth tops to a pair of socks, or they can be made complete from canton flannel. The tunic can be made by following the pattern given on page 5.

The woman's costume illustrated is the one worn during the latter part of the Middle Ages, after the "fitted garment" had been introduced, that is, from the twelfth to the fifteenth century. Its most striking feature is the tall conical headdress, or hennin.

The dresses of this period were made of silk, satin, brocade, or velvet, and were rich and deep in color. Purple, deep blue, crimson, green, or white were commonly used. For costume purposes, the dress may be made of glazed cambric or rayon. In many instances, it will be found possible to fashion it from an old dress. A broad band of ermine encircles the bottom of the skirt and the neck is also trimmed with ermine. This can be reproduced by using cotton wadding and painting in black tails with India ink. The collar effect of revers passing from the center of the waistline in front to the center of the waistline in the back was very popular among the ladies of rank. A piece of rich silk or brocade was worn between the two sides of the collar.

The hennin, or peaked hat, is made of stiff white cambric, covered with silk. The color should harmonize with the dress, but need not match it. White hennins were much worn; but every other color was used including gold and silver. Over the hennin is draped a veil of chiffon or net.

These costumes cover the period of Romeo and Juliet (early 14th century) and can be used for these characters. While Juliet may have worn a hennin in real life, she is generally shown bareheaded, with a filet cap or with a flowing scarf over her hair.


*Yeoman* (Robin Hood and Maid Marian Costume)

The picturesque Robin Hood costume of "Lincoln green" is a perennial favorite and is not difficult to reproduce. Essentially, it is the costume worn by the English yeomen from the twelfth through the fourteenth centuries.

MAID
MARIAN

ROBIN
HOOD

NOBLEWOMAN

NOBLE
IN
ARMOR

NOBLEMAN

PAULDRON

FALD

VIZOR

RERE BRACE

BREAST PLATE
ELBOW COP
VAMBRACE

GAUNTLET

TACES

TASSET

FALD

CUISHE

KNEECOP

WINGS

GREAVE

LATE   MIDDLE   AGES

The long tights can most easily be made from a union suit dyed green, and the tall soft shoes with rolled-over tops can be made by using a pair of men's socks, turning over the tops. They may be either green or brown.

The tunic is made of green cloth or flannel. Follow the pattern for a short tunic given on page 5. It has a broad, loose collar with scalloped edges, which may be either green or brown. It is laced up the front with brown cord to simulate rawhide. Around the waist is a broad brown leather belt.

The archer's hat with its rakish feather can be made of green cloth or crepe paper. A leathern pouch is slung by a strap over the left shoulder and hangs at the right side. Both pouch and strap can be made of brown cloth.

The Maid Marian costume is that worn by the peasant women of England and the Continent from the twelfth through the sixteenth centuries. As Maid Marian was a member of Robin Hood's band, however, the colors used for her costume are green and brown, whereas the peasant women of the time generally wore blue, black, brown, or gray.

The dress and stockings are brown, and the head-covering, belt, pouch and shoes are green. The cloth used for such costumes in medieval times was serge. This can be imitated by using cambric (dull side outwards) or plain challis.

Instead of the headdress shown in the illustration, Maid Marian may wear the peaked cap used by Robin Hood and his men.


*Peasant*

The Robin Hood costume can be used, with minor alterations, for the costume of a medieval peasant or serf of the period from the twelfth to the fourteenth centuries. Omit the cap, collar, belt, and pouch, and make the costume of dark brown or blue serge, or woolen batiste or canton flannel to imitate serge.

The Maid Marian costume is that worn by the peasant women during the late Middle Ages, and until as late as 1500. It is a good one to use for such a play as "The Pied Piper" and for Cinderella's costume before going to the ball.

The costume is also correct without the head covering, for a

Joan of Arc costume. For this purpose, it should be gray or brown in color.

Good books to consult for further details of medieval dress include Boutet de Monvel's "Jeanne d'Arc," "The Modern Reader's Chaucer" by Tatlock and Mackaye, and Guizot's "History of France."

# SIXTEENTH CENTURY EUROPE AND
# ELIZABETHAN ENGLAND

THE general features of the dress of the noble or well-to-do men of the sixteenth century or Elizabethan period is familiar to almost everyone, for it was the dress of Sir Walter Raleigh, Sir Francis Drake, and a host of other well known men of the time. The costumes illustrated, both for men and women, are those that were worn in France and most of the rest of Europe during the same period. The children wore exactly the same type of clothes as their elders.

The man's costume illustrated is suitable not only for such characters as the Elizabethan explorers and courtiers, but also for Columbus, Shakespeare, King Henry VIII, Charles I and James I of England, Richelieu and Francis I of France. It is also the conventional costume for a fairy tale Prince or King.

The woman's costume is suitable for Mary Queen of Scots, Queen Elizabeth and the ladies of her court, Catharine di Medici, and also for Cinderella at the ball and for a fairy tale Queen.

The breeches, doublet, and "Spanish" cape of the man's costume were made of brocade or velvet. Cretonne and deep colored canton flannel make excellent substitutes for these materials. The colors were rich and varied, purple, black, blue, green, and brown being some of the more commonly used. The suit (breeches and doublet), cloak, shoes and stockings, which were more properly tights, were generally of the same color. The cape was usually lined with satin of a contrasting color, which was often brilliant, as scarlet or orange. The doublet was frequently slashed with a contrasting color. The effect of the slashes can be imitated by sewing strips of bright-colored material to the doublet. A narrow leather belt encircles the waist and supports the indispensable sword. The shoes of this period were made of soft leather or velvet. They can be reproduced with velvet, canton flannel or rayon. The ruff was made of sheer lawn, and can be reproduced with gauze. The hat was of velvet and was adorned with a short white plume. It can be made from crepe paper and should match the suit and cape in color.

Long women's stockings, a pair of tights, or the drawers of a union suit may be used for the man's hose. The very short puffed-out breeches can be made from a pair of boy's knickerbockers or

COURT
DRESS

ELIZABETHAN

16TH
CENTURY

from a pair of shorts by gathering in the lower edges of each leg. If this is done, sew elastic around each leg to hold the breeches in place. Many people will prefer to make their own breeches and this can be done very easily by following the pattern shown on page 5. A flannel pyjama top, dyed, and fitted with a ruff, is suggested for the doublet. The cape is easily made by using the semi-circular pattern given on page 5. If the costume is only to be used once, the cape may be made from crepe paper.

The costume of the sixteenth century lady of fashion was characterized by a flowing skirt that was divided in the front to reveal a petticoat of contrasting color, a tight-fitting bodice with narrow sleeves puffed at the shoulder or long full sleeves, and an upstanding fan-shaped lace collar. This type of costume, however, was only worn with a court costume. In house dresses, the bodice was high-necked and was finished off with a ruff that encircled the neck or else had a plain neck. Noble ladies and royalty such as Queen Elizabeth wore farthingales beneath their skirts which made the latter practically as full as hoop-skirts. They also favored the long stomacher that is shown in the illustration of the court dress.

Any colors desired may be used for the dress and petticoat. Effective combinations are a pink, blue or yellow petticoat with a black, red or dark blue dress. The dress was frequently made of brocade. This can be reproduced with cretonne or cotton tapestry. The petticoats frequently had a border of contrasting color. The puffs at the shoulders were slashed with a different color from the dress. The sleeves were finished at the wrists with ruffles of gauze.

The skirt can be made on a wire and tape hoop-skirt foundation (see page 5) or can be supported by a farthingale (see page 5) and held out at the bottom by a wire stitched into the hem. For a costume that is not designed for permanency, crepe paper is excellent material to use for the skirt and petticoat. The bodice can be made by following the pattern shown on page 5. It is worth while to look around the house, however, to see if there is not an old velvet dress than can be used with the addition of full long sleeves. If a stomacher is needed for a Queen Elizabeth or court costume, it can be made from buckram covered with the same material as that from which the rest of the costume is made and decorated with crepe paper "embroidery."

*Peasant*

The costume worn by peasants, or by men who were not nobles, was practically the same as that worn by the nobles but of coarser materials. Serge was used for the breeches and doublet and instead of a ruff, the peasant wore a linen collar or no collar. No peasant, moreover, ever wore the jaunty short cloak. The yeoman or man-at-arms wore a leather jerkin or tunic over an unbleached linen shirt with puffed sleeves.

Peasant women wore a costume similar to the Maid Marian costume, but without the head covering, girdle or pouch. The blouse should have a round low-cut neck, and an apron may be worn, for it was during the sixteenth century that the apron first came into use.

Children's costumes in the sixteenth century, both rich and poor, were of the same type as those worn by the adults, and can be made by following the directions given for the adult's costumes. From 1500 on, boys wore doublet and hose. The girl's costume from 1500 to 1600 should be without the hanging sleeves and the bodice should be longer and pointed. From 1600 to 1700 the costume is the same except for the bodice, which should be long and not pointed.

There are dozens of history books and biographies that contain pictures of the well-known people of the Elizabethan era. These will be found helpful to provide details of specific costumes that may be required. The costumes of this period are also shown in the paintings of Holbein and Dürer, copies of which are obtainable at most libraries.

## SEVENTEENTH CENTURY EUROPE
## AND AMERICA

THE illustrations show the costumes worn by the 17th century Cavaliers of the Three Musketeers type and by the courtiers and noblemen of England and France. These costumes are suitable not only for Cavaliers and courtiers of the period, but also for the monarchs such as Charles I of England and Louis XIV of France. It is also the costume for Cyrano de Bergerac, and do not forget to add his long upturned nose.

The Cavalier's breeches are tan, red, blue, green, purple, or any other bright color. They can be made from pyjama trousers cut off, with a frill added below the knee. A fuller pair of breeches can be made from gymnasium bloomers. The doublet is of the same color as the breeches, and can be fashioned from a pyjama top. The shirt has a wide white collar, edged with lace, and frilly lace cuffs. The velvet cape should be of some bright solid color or colors, such as blue or purple, lined with red. It is made from a square piece of material. The materials used in the Cavaliers' costumes were silk, velvet, and cloth. Sateen is a good substitute for silk, and canton flannel for velvet.

The wide boot-tops so characteristic of this period can be made of buckram covered with brown cloth, or of enamel cloth. These tops are slipped on over the shoes and held in place by a strap passing under the instep. The Cavalier's broad-brimmed, plumed hat can be made by adding a buckram brim covered with brown sateen to an ordinary felt hat.

The courtier or nobleman's costume is of the type worn toward the end of the seventeenth century. The materials were now silk or satin, and the colors were white and delicate blues, pinks, and yellows. The breeches were narrower than those worn by the Cavaliers and had lace ruffles at the knee encircled by gayly-colored ribbons. The long waistcoat was of figured brocade and reached almost to the knees. It can be faked by sewing two long rectangular pieces of material to the front of an ordinary vest. The coat had three-quarter length sleeves with broad cuffs formed by turning back the end of the sleeve and facing the turned-back part with brocade. Probably the best way to make the coat is to use an old suit coat as a base. Sew cloth or crepe paper over it to give the extra length, cover up the lapels, and add extra fullness to the

COURTIER

CAVALIER

17TH
CENTURY

sleeves. An amusing touch can be added to the costume by having the wearer carry a muff attached to a belt. All men of fashion in England and France carried muffs from 1688 until nearly the end of the century.

The outstanding features of women's dress in seventeenth century England and France were the very full skirt, which was worn with an over-skirt, and the round-necked, tight bodice with puffed sleeves. The costume can be made from taffeta or satin. The underskirt is either figured or plain; the overskirt is of contrasting material. The bodice is made of the same material as the overskirt and comes to a sharp point at the waistline. The broad collar is of pointed lace and there is a bow of colored ribbon where the collar fastens. The cuffs on the sleeves are also of pointed lace.

Feather fans were extremely popular during this period, and jewelry, often of colored glass, was worn in abundance. Stockings were frequently of scarlet, light blue, or apple-green silk, and slippers were equally gay, popular colors being red, blue, violet and yellow.

Children wore the same costumes as their elders, the boys wearing knee-breeches, lace-trimmed shirts and doublets, and the girls wearing dresses that came to the floor.

## Puritans

The Puritans' costume was a simplified version of the clothing worn in England at the time of their departure for America. All fripperies like ribbons, laces and feathers were, of course, frowned upon. Essentially, it was the costume worn by the Roundheads or followers of Oliver Cromwell. It is the costume to use for Priscilla and John Alden and, with the minor variations described, for Elizabethan and Roundhead soldiers, Miles Standish, and Captain John Smith.

The colors used by the Puritans were, however, much warmer and richer than is generally realized. Favored colors for the men's knee-breeches were dark brown, dark blue, black, and a deep brown orange. The woolen stockings were dark gray, green, or blue. They were fastened below the knee by black ribbons.

The same colors were used for the doublets as for the breeches. Indispensable features of these garments were the large white collar, called the "playne band," and the turned-back cuffs of Holland

PURITAN SOLDIER

PURITAN and INDIAN

linen. From the shoulders hung a short cape or mantle. The Puritan's costume was completed by the tall broad-brimmed hat of black felt. This can be reproduced by covering a cardboard framework with black cloth or crepe paper. A suit of flannel pyjamas, suitably altered and dyed, is suggested for the breeches and doublet.

The Puritan women wore gowns of purple, gray, and russet material. Over the skirt was a large apron of white linen. The stockings were of black wool and the shoes were of heavy black leather.

When going outdoors the Puritan woman threw a large white kerchief around her shoulders, fastening it in front with a brooch. In really cold weather a close-fitting hood of dark cloth was a necessary part of the outdoor costume. The hood worn in wintertime was trimmed with fur, while the hood worn in warmer weather was edged with a narrow band of white linen.

Some of the Pilgrims and Puritans wore light body-armor of the type shown in the drawing. This uniform, with slight variations, is also correct for Elizabethan and Roundhead soldiers, and for Miles Standish and Captain John Smith.

Under the armor is worn a tunic and breeches of brown or blue serge. Use knickerbockers for the breeches and an ordinary shirt for the tunic as only the sleeves show. The tunic has a ruff of lawn at the neck. The armor and helmet are made of buckram covered with aluminum paint or silver paper. The leather shoulder straps and fastenings at the waist can be made from brown cloth.

The Elizabethan soldier wears the exact costume shown, but has breeches of red slashed with blue or yellow.

Miles Standish, Puritan soldiers and Roundhead soldiers wear brown tunic and breeches and have the broad Puritan collar instead of a ruff. The armor is the same.

Captain John Smith should have a plum-colored tunic and breeches and should wear knee boots instead of shoes and stockings. His armor is the same as that shown in the drawing.

### American Indian

Before the arrival of the white men, the principal article of clothing worn by the Indian braves was a simply-made leather breech cloth. Within a very short space of time. however, the Indians adopted trousers and hunting shirts and it is this latter costume that is most frequently associated with them. The costume illustrated is patterned after one worn by a chief of the Blackfeet, one of the largest and most powerful of the Northern plains tribes.

The fringed deerskin leggings can be reproduced by using a pair of khaki trousers, or a pair of pyjama trousers dyed tan-color. The fringe is made of a three-inch strip of brown material. At intervals of one-half inch, make cuts two and a half inches deep. This leaves a one-half inch band for attaching. To the side of each leg, just in front of the fringe, is sewed a strip of white cloth about twenty inches long and three inches wide. This is marked with red ink and India ink to represent an Indian beadwork design.

The feet should be encased in Indian moccasins. These are generally obtainable, but if a pair cannot be found, they can be reproduced in brown denim.

The imitation deerskin hunting shirt is made from cambric (unglazed side outward) or denim. The shirt is cut on straight lines, and consists simply of two rectangular pieces of cloth sewed together with a hole cut in the top for the neck opening. This should be just large enough for the wearer's head to slip through. Full length sleeves are added to complete the garment. The shirt should reach halfway to the wearer's knees and should be fringed at the bottom and at the cuffs of the sleeves.

A realistic touch can be added by sewing a number of "scalps" to the front of the shirt. These were not necessarily the scalps of enemies. An Indian frequently used locks of his own or his wife's hair. Each lock represented some *coup* such as saving a friend's life, being wounded, taking a prisoner, or capturing a horse. Hair for the scalps can be obtained by buying black switches at the ten-cent store. The shirt may be further decorated with strips of imitation bead work sewed to the sleeves and to the front on each side of the neck opening.

Around the neck are hung several strings of beads. These can be made or borrowed from campfire organizations. To complete the chief's costume, a feather headdress should be worn. One of these can be made at home by following the design shown in the drawing. Make a close-fitting cap and sew around it a band of buckram about an inch wide. Sew the feathers that surround the head to the buckram and cover their lower ends with a band of red or buff canton flannel. Make the tail-piece by sewing a number of feathers to a long strip of buckram. When all the feathers are in place sew a strip of red or buff canton flannel along each side of the buckram, and stitch the tail-piece to the feathered cap. If it is impossible to obtain the feathers needed for a headdress, they can be obtained together with the other materials needed, from the headquarters of the Boy Scouts of America.

The women of the Plains Indian tribes wore a costume consisting of deerskin leggings and moccasins, a straight-cut knee-length gown of the same material, and a beaded belt.

The leggings can be reproduced with khaki trousers or pyjama trousers, decorated with imitation bead work, like those of the man.

The gown, or tunic, is made in the same way as the man's hunting shirt, but is longer. The sleeves, however, are only elbow-length. The bottom of the tunic is deeply fringed. The beaded belt is made of cloth painted in imitation of an Indian design.

Like the men, the women wore many bead necklaces. The hair was divided in the middle and braided, the braids being wrapped with strips of red cloth. In addition, many of the women wore a beaded headband.

Hiawatha actually wore a loin cloth, as he lived before the white men came. For plays, however, he is generally costumed in the later form of Indian costume that is illustrated.

Pocahontas wears the costume illustrated, but traditionally it is made of white doeskin. This can be imitated by using white canton flannel.

## EIGHTEENTH CENTURY EUROPE AND
## AMERICAN COLONIAL

THE American colonial gentleman of the eighteenth century wore the garments of the French man of fashion and this style was also in vogue in England. The same situation prevailed in connection with American colonial woman's dress. The costumes illustrated and described can, consequently, be used to represent eighteenth century French and English men and women as well as those of Colonial America. The men's costumes are suitable for George Washington, Benjamin Franklin, Nathan Hale, Lafayette, George II, George III, Monsieur Beaucaire, and Louis XV. Those of the women can be used for Martha Washington, Betsy Ross, Molly Pitcher, Marie Antoinette, Madame du Barry, and Catharine the Great. These costumes are correct for such plays as "She Stoops to Conquer," "School for Scandal," and "The Rivals." They are also the costumes to be worn by a so-called "Dresden" shepherd and shepherdess.

Favorite colors for the cotton or wool knee-breeches, waistcoat, and long full-skirted coat were black, blue, brown, green and plum. On dress occasions these garments were made of silk, satin or brocade and were frequently very gay in color—white knee-breeches, for example, with coat and waistcoat of pink, light blue or yellow.

Patterns from which to make both the man's and the woman's costumes, can be obtained at the department stores and in most instances, it will save time and energy to use such a pattern as a guide. The material used for the man's garments should be cambric or sateen. The stockings are of white silk, and the shoes are of black leather with tall tongues and large silver buckles. The tongues can be made from black cloth paper. If a woman's riding hat of the right type is obtainable, it should be used for the man's tricorn hat. Otherwise an imitation can be made by sewing black cloth over a buckram framework.

The principal features of the woman's costume are the quilted petticoat, the Watteau overdress, and the perky little white cap. The petticoats were usually made of light solid colored silk or satin— pink, blue, white, or yellow. They were filled with a layer of cotton or wadding and then run with stitches in quilt fashion to hold the wadding in place. This quilting does not have to be duplicated in a costume.

Over the petticoat was worn the Watteau overdress of chintz or dimity. It was generally made of striped or flowered material. On dress occasions the overdress was made of flowered silk or brocade. When allowed to touch the floor, as was sometimes done, the overdress trailed out behind for several feet. Generally, however, it was worn looped up as shown in the drawing. Around the neck of the overdress was worn a dainty white muslin fichu. White stockings were worn with black slippers adorned with silver buckles. The little cap was made of the finest gauze and was trimmed with lace. It became popular prior to the Revolution and remained in fashion for nearly half a century. This is the costume worn by a "Dresden" shepherdess.

The more elaborate hoop-skirted dress illustrated was that worn by French and English noble women and ladies of the court and also by American women on formal occasions. It was usually made of a light-colored brocade of flowers or ribbons, or of striped material. Narrow ruffles at the neck line, down the front of the bodice and the sides of the overskirt and across the bottom of the underskirt were very popular. These formal costumes were made of silk and brocaded satins, which can be imitated with mercerized poplins, rayon, and light weight cambric.

### Quakers

The Quaker men wore practically the same costume as other men of the period—long coat, vest and knee-breeches of brown or plum-colored wool, broadcloth or cotton flannel, black stockings, shoes and hat, and a lace and linen neck cloth. The hat was of the broad-brimmed type made familiar by the many pictures of William Penn.

Quaker women were far more simply garbed than the ladies of the gay world. Their costume consisted of a gray wool or poplin dress with a white apron and a white kerchief about the shoulders. On their heads they wore a black poke bonnet over an underbonnet of white lace or sheer lawn. This costume is not illustrated, as pictures of it can be found in any library, by looking up the William Penn period.

AMERICAN
COLONIAL

FORMAL
DRESS

18TH
CENTURY

### American Minute Man

Use the man's ordinary costume without the coat for an American Minute Man. The costume will then consist of knee-breeches and a white shirt, with or without a waistcoat. A three-cornered hat, a powder horn slung over the shoulder, and an old-fashioned musket complete the costume. If desired, tan gaiters may be worn over the stockings.

### George Washington's Soldiers

The infantrymen, who are usually represented in plays and pageants wore the knee-breeches, waistcoats, and long coats of the period costume. The breeches were buff or tan and were sometimes worn with stockings, sometimes with gaiters. Waistcoats were buff or white. The coats were blue with white buttons and lined in white. New York and New Jersey troops had buff facings, New England troops white facings, and Virginia, Pennsylvania, Maryland and Delaware troops red facings.

### George Washington

When portrayed as a young man in his days as a surveyor, Washington should wear the pioneer's costume with an imitation deer-skin cap. As a civilian before and after the Revolution, he should wear the costume illustrated in gray, buff or plum for ordinary wear, and with white breeches and vest and blue coat for formal occasions. The formal costume, with gold trimmings on the coat and gold epaulettes, is correct for Washington as commander of the Army.

### British Officer and Soldier

The British officer wears white breeches and waistcoat, a jabot and stock, and a scarlet coat. The coat has gold buttons and epaulettes, and white ruffles are sewed to the cuffs. The hat is red or black with gold braid around the edge. The boots are of black leather and should be fitted with spurs.

The original material of the breeches, waistcoat and coat was generally broadcloth, which can be imitated by using canton flannel.

The soldier wears scarlet broadcloth (canton flannel) breeches

PIONEER WOMAN

PIONEER

AMERICAN SAILOR

BRITISH SAILOR

BRITISH OFFICER

BRITISH SOLDIER

AMERICAN REVOLUTION

and coat and a white waistcoat. The front of the coat is faced with dark green cloth trimmed with white braid and buttons. Sometimes the breeches were white. The legs may be clad in white stockings or black leggings. Two white bands cross the soldier's chest and fasten at shoulders and hips. The hat is black and is made by sewing cloth over a buckram foundation.

### American and British Sailors

The uniform worn by the American sailor has not altered very noticeably during the century and a half since the Navy was founded, and the costume illustrated is suitable for all periods, with slight modifications as noted below.

The bell-shaped trousers of the present-day costume are somewhat difficult to make, though they will present no difficulties to anyone who is clever at designing and sewing. They can be "faked" by sewing bell-shaped bottoms to the legs of a pair of blue overall trousers. The blouse is also difficult to make at home, and it is best to use a ready-made gymnasium blouse dyed dark blue. The hat can be made by sewing dark blue cloth over a buckram foundation.

The sailor's trousers at the time of the Revolution did not flare as much as they do today. Ordinary blue serge trousers or overall trousers can be used to reproduce them. The hats were more crumpled, as they were worn without the grommet that keeps them flat today.

The British tar has always worn a uniform very similar to that of his American cousin—bell-shaped trousers, and a blouse with a square sailor collar. His hat during the Revolution and the War of 1812, however, was of the shiny black circular-crowned type shown in the drawing. The costume illustrated is good for "Pinafore," but it should be the summer costume of white material instead of the heavier blue winter uniform.

Sir Joseph Porter in "Pinafore" would wear the eighteenth century costume with white silk knee-breeches, a blue coat with gold braid, and a cocked hat.

### Pioneers

The costume of Daniel Boone and the other early pioneers and trappers is one in which every American has a particular interest, for it is one of the few distinctive costumes that have originated in this country. While the original garments were made of dressed deerskins, they can be reproduced by using khaki or tan-colored flannel.

The fringed leggings or drawers can be made from flannel pyjama trousers dyed brown or tan. Make the fringe as described on page 103 for the Indian costume. Indian moccasins should be worn, but if these are not obtainable, their place can be taken by brown shoes.

The hunting shirt, or tunic, can be made by sewing a short fringed skirt to an ordinary khaki shirt, and adding a fringed circular collar. It is held in at the waist by a narrow leather belt to which is attached a bullet-pouch and, if obtainable, a powder horn and hunting knife.

The coonskin cap can be reproduced by covering a circular cardboard or buckram frame with dark brown sateen and attaching an imitation raccoon's tail made of cotton. The cotton is dyed brown and the black circles are marked on with black paint or India ink. If the coonskin cap is not used, the pioneer may wear a low-crowned, broad-brimmed hat of black or brown felt. This can be made by covering a buckram foundation with flannelette or cambric, with the dull side out.

The pioneer woman wears a simple gray or brown homespun dress with a tight waist and a fairly full skirt gathered in pleats at the waist. If the dress is specially made, the material may be woolen batiste, flannelette, or cambric, dull side out. A white or checkered apron is tied around the waist, and a woolen shawl, or white kerchief, is fastened around the shoulders. The head may be uncovered or protected by a cap of the type shown in the illustration.

## EARLY NINETEENTH CENTURY
## OR EMPIRE PERIOD

THE clothes worn during the Empire Period, or from 1800 to about 1830, were those with which we are familiar through pictures of Napoleon and Josephine. Although these costumes originated in France, they were adopted in England and America and were worn with but slight variation in both these countries during the early nineteenth century. The costume is correct for characters of the period, such as Beau Brummel and Lafayette, and for characters in Dickens' stories laid in the early part of the century, such as Mister McCawber in *David Copperfield* and the adults in *Oliver Twist* and *The Christmas Carol;* for Becky Sharp and characters in *Vanity Fair* and Jane Austen's *Pride and Prejudice.* Men wore either long tight-fitting breeches that reached to the ankle and fastened with a strap under the instep, or tight knee breeches and stockings. The long breeches can be reproduced by using a pair of tights or long winter underdrawers. White was the usual color. The usual footwear consisted of short boots or pumps.

Stocks were worn about the neck, and the waistcoats were short, ending in a straight line at the waist. The coat was of the cutaway type and had either a wide collar or a high, turned-over collar. A good way to reproduce this garment is to use an old dress-suit coat. The hat is a beaver with a straight or bell crown.

The popular colors during the Empire Period were dark green, blue, mustard yellow, buff and black. Any one of these is suitable for the man's waistcoat and coat. Woolen cloth was the material most in use.

The women's dresses were high-waisted and had short puffed sleeves and long skirts. Party dresses were made of silk, satin, and silk muslin, while plain muslin or cotton was used for everyday wear. The colors were the same as those favored by the men. Sprigged muslin was also widely used.

The women's slippers resembled sandals and had ribbons that sometimes passed over the instep and sometimes were laced for some distance above the ankle. Long gloves or lace mitts were an almost indispensable part of the costume, and light scarfs were much worn.

There were many different kinds of hats, but the poke bonnet was the most usually worn and the hat most generally associated with the period.

EARLY 19TH
CENTURY

KATE
GREENAWAY
COSTUMES

# FIRST EMPIRE

The children of this period wore the clothes that have come to be known as the "Kate Greenaway" costume. This costume was worn in America, England and France and is suitable for plays of the early 19th Century and *The Christmas Carol* of Dickens. In costuming any Dickens characters, it is well to refer to a well illustrated edition of the book in question, for details of the costume. The Kate Greenaway costume is correct also for many Mother Goose characters such as Miss Muffett, Mistress Mary, Little Boy Blue, Tom the Piper's Son, and Jack and Jill.

The costumes are easy to cut out and put together and in many cases can be made by altering slightly children's clothes already on hand. The materials used for the girls' dresses were silk and muslin; while the boys' clothes were of satin, or woolen cloth. The colors were always soft and light such as pale blue, light yellow, pink, white and pale green.

## MID-VICTORIAN ENGLAND AND AMERICAN CIVIL WAR PERIOD

These costumes are frequently needed for historical tableaux and pageants, and for plays of the Lincoln period such as *Little Women, Secret Service,* and *Captain Jinks.* The man's costume is of the type worn in America, England, Ireland, and France, during the 1860's. The woman's costume is suitable for Barbara Frietche. Both are correct for any play about Lincoln. Abraham Lincoln himself wore the man's costume and also frequently wore a shawl. Pictures of him can be found at any library for verification of minor details.

The man's trousers are a little narrower than most of those worn today and are worn uncreased and without cuffs. The vest is cut lower than modern-day waistcoats, and frequently had lapels. Both of these garments, however, can be reproduced by using their present-day counterparts. The long coat is a different matter. It can be made by re-modeling a discarded overcoat, but the best plan is to make one. The most widely used colors were black, gray, and dark blue. Make the trousers and vest gray or fawn-colored, and the coat black or blue.

COWBOY

SOLDIER

CIVIL WAR
PERIOD

The distinguishing feature of the woman's costume is the enormous hoop-skirt, which is supported by a wire frame. The full-sleeved blouse is almost entirely covered by a jacket that fastens with cords across the front. Favored materials were silk, satin, and poplin. Colors were as varied as today. Evening dresses had hoop-skirts and various types of bodices, that were frequently very elaborate. They were made of bright colored silk, satin, tarlatan, or silk muslin. The little girl's costume has a wide skirt and a distinctive jacket that was peculiar to the Civil War period. Details of the frame for the hoop-skirt are shown on page 5.

Little boys of the Civil War period wore long, uncreased trousers, white shirts with full sleeves, and jackets of the same type as those worn by the little girls.

The Civil War Soldiers' uniform is made of blue material for Northern soldiers and of gray for Southern soldiers. Blue overalls or old gray flannel slacks can be used for the trousers. For the blouse use a Boy Scout or army tunic covered with blue or gray cloth. The forage cap is made by covering a buckram foundation with cloth of the proper color.

### Cowboy

The western cowboy who was so picturesque a figure of the late nineteenth century developed a distinctive costume.

The cowboy's chaps can be made from a pair of khaki trousers. They are "disguised" by the addition of cloth "wings" sewed to the outside seam at the bottom of each leg and by the covering of "fur." This can be imitated by using Turkish toweling dyed brown.

The cowboy wears a checked shirt, a kerchief knotted around his neck, and a short buttonless vest of heavy cloth or leather. The vest may be made of canton flannel or denim or can be made from an old waistcoat. A "ten gallon" hat, or the nearest approach to one that can be obtained, a lariat made from clothes line, and a dummy gun and holster, complete the costume.

# PART III

# SPECIAL COSTUMES

# FANCIFUL COSTUMES

HERE is a group of frequently used fanciful costumes: Pierrot and Pierrette, the traditional Clown, Harlequin, the Jester, an animal or two, Santa Claus, and the Hallowe'en ghost.

*Pierrot* wears a loose, baggy clown costume of white cloth with black spots. His ruff is white and can be made by pleating a five-inch strip of stiff muslin or crepe paper and sewing it to a neckband. His hat, made of cloth-covered buckram, is white with a black pompon at one side. Pierrot's face is usually chalk-white. The suit can be made of white muslin, rayon, or inexpensive cotton material. If needed, a pattern can be purchased at any department store.

*Pierrette* wears a simple white dress with a rather full skirt that is decorated with large black or red polka dots. These may be made of crepe paper or cloth. A stiff white muslin or crepe paper ruff encircles her neck and she wears a white hat with the same color polka dots as those on her dress.

The *Clown's* costume is the same as that worn by Pierrot, but should have red polka dots instead of black. His face should be whitened, and there should be a big red circle on each cheek.

*Harlequin* wears an unromantic union suit which is given a carnival appearance by covering it with gay diamond-patterned material. An indispensable part of his costume is the black mask.

The *Jester's* costume, with its cap and bells, may be made by combining a pair of long underdrawers with a pyjama top. The legs of the drawers, or tights, are parti-colored, and the doublet has striped sleeves and a checkerboard pattern. The bottom of the doublet is divided into points and to each point is attached a little brass bell. Another bell is fastened to the pointed hood.

*Animals*—The basis for most animal costumes is a suit of woolen or flannel pyjamas, or else a one-piece sleeping garment. Paws made of flannel are sewed to both legs and sleeves or to the legs alone if the wearer must use his hands. For a wolf or dog costume, the pyjamas should be dyed brown and a cloth or crepe paper tail should be added. The head, except for the face, is covered with a close-fitting hood, and a mask representing the proper animal must be worn, as it is very difficult to "fake" an animal's features from cloth or other ordinary materials.

GHOST

HARLEQUIN

PIERRETTE

SANTA CLAUS

PIERROT

JESTER

FANCIFUL COSTUME

The rabbit's ears are made from canton flannel or white crepe paper stretched around frames made of wire, buckram or cardboard.

*Ghost*—The ghost's costume is easy to make, for it may be either an inexpensive white domino with hood attached, or a sheet draped over the head and around the body, held in place by a cord around the waist. An essential part of the costume, of course, is the death's-head mask. This can be purchased at the ten-cent store or made at home from white muslin. Cut holes for the eyes and nose and mark around each with black. Draw a mouth with large teeth, in the correct position.

*Santa Claus*—The most practical way to make a home-made Santa Claus costume is to employ our old friend—a pair of pyjamas. Dye both coat and trousers red. The trousers require no alterations at all, but they should be ample enough to give a baggy appearance. The boots can be "faked" by wearing ordinary black shoes and covering the legs with black oilcloth, or rubber boots may be worn.

The tunic is trimmed down the front, round the hem, and at the cuffs of the sleeves with white cotton to represent fur. Beneath it there should be a pillow or two to give the wearer the traditional rotundity of Santa Claus. A broad, black leather belt with a big buckle is an indispensable part of the traditional costume. Be sure to make it large enough to include the pillow.

Santa Claus's cap is easily made from red flannel trimmed with white cotton. If desired, little brass bells can be sewed to the cuffs of the sleeves and the hem of the tunic, to jingle as Santa Claus walks about.


## FAIRY TALE COSTUMES

HERE are a number of fairy tale costumes that are in constant demand for children's plays and parties.

*Witch*—The witch costume, with minor variations and the use of different colors, is also suitable for a Wicked Fairy, The Sleeping Beauty, a Fairy Godmother (Cinderella), Mother Goose, Old Mother Hubbard, and the Old Woman Who Lived in a Shoe. Cambric and woolen batiste are good materials to use, and, for a less substantial costume, crepe paper. The crown of the hat is made of buckram and the brim of cardboard.

PIRATE

DWARF

ELF

FAIRY

PETER PAN

WITCH

FAIRY TALE

The witch has an orange skirt with black panniers, a black bodice, and a black cape that may be lined with orange if desired. The hat is solid black. This costume is needed most frequently for presentations of the ever popular "Hansel and Gretel" by McLaren.

*The Wicked Fairy* wears the same costume as the Witch, but may be all in black, or have red instead of orange.

*The Fairy Godmother* wears a red shirt and panniers and a dark green bodice and cape. The hat is red with a black brim.

*Mother Goose* traditionally wears a red quilted skirt with white or gray panniers, a black bodice, and a black or gray cape lined with red. Her hat is gray or brown and has a flat top, not a pointed one.

*Old Mother Hubbard* should wear a skirt of flowered material, red panniers, a black bodice, and a blue or green cape. Instead of the pointed hat, she has a white mob-cap. On her hands she wears black knitted mitts.

*Fairy*—The fairy's dress is made of white cheese-cloth, chiffon, rayon, or crepe paper. Traditionally, it has crossed ribbons in the Greek manner over the chest. The wings can be made of cardboard, or of white muslin stretched over a wire frame. Sew them to a broad band of the material of which the dress is made and bring the ends of the band around to the front, *underneath* the dress, tying or pinning firmly.

Note:—This costume, without the wings, is correct for a girl of ancient Greece and a girl of ancient Rome. The colors may be white, blue, yellow, or brick red.

*Elf or Brownie*—This costume can be made very simply by dyeing a union suit the proper color, green for an elf, or brown for a brownie. The long, pointed shoes are made of canvas or buckram covered with cloth. The peaked cap is made of cambric, canton flannel, or crepe paper.

*Dwarf*—For "Snow White and the Seven Dwarfs," "Rip van Winkle," and other fairy plays. The dwarf wears red or brown tights ending in long pointed shoes of the same color. The tights may be the lower part of a union suit and the shoes are made in the same way as those of the elf. The doublet is green with a red or brown collar and can be made from a pyjama top. The addition of the collar and broad belt, together with the change of color, will make the original garment unrecognizable. The long stocking-cap is made of red or green canton flannel.

*Peter Pan's* costume is very similar to that worn by the dwarf. Its color scheme is green and brown, the shoes are not pointed, and the hat is of the Robin Hood type with a feather.

*Pirate*—This is the costume needed in "Peter Pan," "Treasure Island," "Captain Kidd," and "The Pirates of Penzance." The knee-breeches and long coat are black or dark green, the shirt is white, and the stockings red. The cuffs of the coat sleeves are turned back and faced with red flannel and a red or blue sash encircles the waist. The boot tops are made from black oilcloth or buckram covered with cloth. A lady's tricorn riding hat can be used for the pirate's hat but if one of these is not available, the hat can be made from buckram covered with black flannel. A red bandanna may be tied around the head beneath the hat. Earrings made from brass curtain rings and dummy pistols and cutlasses thrust into the sash, complete the costume.

The Index,

usually occupying this position, has been placed in the front of the book, immediately following the Table of Contents, to serve as a list of suggestions of costumes for pageants and masquerades.

## DATE DUE

| | | | |
|---|---|---|---|
| | | | |
| | | | |
| | | | |
| | | | |
| | | | |
| | | | |
| | | | |
| | | | |
| | | | |
| | | | |
| | | | |
| | | | |
| | | | |
| | | | |
| | | | |
| D | | | PRINTED IN U.S.A. |